Create a Web site

for beginners

Rob Young

WHSMITH LTD, SWINDON, WILTS. SN3 3LD
In association with:

PEARSON EDUCATION LIMITED
Head Office:
Edinburgh Gate, Harlow, Essex CM20 2JE
Tel: +44 (0)1279 623623 Fax: +44 (0)1279 431059

London Office:
128 Long Acre, London WC2E 9AN
Tel: +44 (0)20 7447 2000 Fax: +44 (0)20 7240 5771
Website: www.it-minds.com

First published in Great Britain 2001
© Pearson Education Limited 2001

British Library Cataloguing in Publication Data
A CIP catalogue record for this book can be obtained from the British Library

ISBN 0-130-65279-2

10 9 8 7 6 5 4

Typeset by Pantek Arts Ltd, Maidstone, Kent.
Printed and bound in Great Britain by Ashford Colour Press, Gosport, Hampshire.

The publishers' policy is to use paper manufactured from sustainable forests.

contents

introduction

From the moment you start surfing the World Wide Web, you realise it's unique. After all, where else can you find a never-ending supply of information, entertainment and services, all instantly available from the comfort of your own home? But the Web is unique in other ways too, and those tend to sink in a bit more slowly:

● Most of the pages you find on the Web are written by ordinary people like you and me.

● Anyone can put a site on the Web which could potentially be seen by hundreds of millions of people around the world.

● Pages you publish can cover almost any subject you like, and can include pictures, animations, sounds, and interactive tools such as guestbooks and chat rooms.

● A Web site is *dynamic* – you can change it or add to it at any time.

● All this is free! (Okay, there are a few 'extras' that could cost you money if you decide you want them, but if you've got an Internet connection you can get a Web site up and running without paying a single penny.)

In this little book, you'll learn how to design your own Web site using the two building blocks of Web design – a pair of easy-to-use text languages called HTML and CSS. We'll start off simply, with one basic Web page, and gradually introduce new items and features. Along the way you'll find plenty of examples, and I'll point you towards useful sites where you can find extra information, any software you need, and free content to spice up your own site. Finally I'll show you how to get your site on to the Web for the world to see – and how to tell the world it's there!

Throughout the book, we use the following symbols:

These notes provide additional information.

 These notes list shortcuts, advanced techniques, etc.

These notes warn you of pitfalls, and explain how to avoid them.

I've also used different typefaces to make particular meanings clear, as shown below:

Convention	Description
Bold type	Indicates a new term being encountered, or an Internet address
SCRIPT/CODE	Indicates HTML code that you'll type into your own page
ITALIC CODE	In some cases, you'll have to type a particular filename into your HTML code, enter your own email address, or something similar. Italic code-text indicates that you need to replace what I've typed with your own text.

1

Web building basics

- The Web – you use it, you like it, but what is it?
- Learn how URLs work, and how the Web is linked together
- Meet HTML, the 'language' used to write Web pages
- Find out what software you need to build a Web site

A re you the curious type? Have you ever wondered how Web pages are written, how entire sites are constructed, or how the whole lot gets on to the World Wide Web for the rest of us to use? If you have, and you've found the answers, it's time to get that smug look ready. If you haven't, it's because up to now you've never really needed to know: one of the great things about the Web is that you can use it without understanding how it works. You need to know a bit more before you can *write* for the Web, of course, and in this chapter we're going to race through the basics.

Throughout this book I'm going to assume that you have a computer with an Internet connection and you've done some Web surfing. That means you already have the two things you need to get started in Web design, a Web browser and a text editor, but we'll also take a quick look at the other options available.

What is the World Wide Web?

There are two vital things to know about the World Wide Web. The first is that it's a **distributed** system, meaning that it's 'spread around'. Let's take a small example of this first: back in 1995, the first edition of Microsoft's Encarta encyclopaedia was small enough to fit on a single CD-ROM; three years later it had grown to the point that two CDs were needed – in other words, the information had to be *distributed* across two CDs. The Web works in a similar way, except that the CDs are replaced with computers called **Web servers**. When you sign up for an account with almost any Internet service provider (ISP) nowadays, they allocate some space for you on the hard disk of their Web server which is where your finished site will be stored. ISPs all over the world have their own Web servers, so the pages that make up the World Wide Web are *distributed* amongst all these computers. The benefits of this are twofold: first, the Web can never get full; and second, the millions of Web users around the world aren't all connecting to the same computer every time they surf!

The second important thing to know about the Web is that it's based on **hypertext**. Hypertext is a system of clickable text links often used in Windows Help files and multimedia encyclopaedias. It lets you view information in a non-linear way: rather than working in a 'straight line' from page 1 to page 2 to page 3, you may be able to jump from page 1 to a related note on page 57. The Web takes this system a few stages further:

● These links don't have to take you to another point in the same document, or even to another document on the same computer: you can jump to a page on a computer on the other side of the world.

+info

Web server

A server is a computer whose main task in life is to send information to another computer connected to it. On the Internet, those connections are made by telephone lines and modems, but a server could sit in the corner of a small office and be connected to other computers in that office by a mass of cables. Internet servers usually do one particular job: a Web server stores and sends Web pages, an email server holds your email messages until you're ready to retrieve them, and so on.

Create a Web site

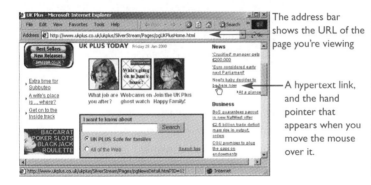

The address bar shows the URL of the page you're viewing

A hypertext link, and the hand pointer that appears when you move the mouse over it.

Figure 1.1

Hypertext links in a typical Web page.

● A hypertext link in a Web page (Fig. 1.1) doesn't have to be a word or phrase: it could be a picture that you click on, or a small part of a larger picture, with different parts linking to different pages (known as an *image map*).

● The link doesn't necessarily open a new Web page: it could play a video or a sound, display a picture, download an application, run a program... The list goes on, and gets longer all the time!

How does hypertext work?

Every file on the World Wide Web has its own unique address, in much the same way as every house in the world has its own street address. This is known as its **URL** (short for Uniform Resource Locator). You've probably come across a lot of these already on your Web wanderings: every time you arrive at a new page, its URL is shown in your browser's address bar. As an example, let's take the URL of the Radio 1 Web site at the BBC and break it up into its component parts. The URL is http://www.bbc.co.uk/radio1/index.html.

http://   This is one of the Internet's many protocols, and it stands for HyperText Transfer Protocol. It's the method Web servers use to transfer Web pages around the Net, so almost all Web page URLs have the http:// prefix.

www.bbc.co.uk/	This is the name of the computer on which the file is stored, identifying one single computer among all the Web servers of the world. Most Web servers' names (though not all) begin with www.
radio1/	This is the directory path to the page we want to open. Just as on your own computer, the path may consist of several directory names separated by slashes. Most Web designers structure their sites so that different areas are in different directories with intuitive names: the BBC site also has directories called **radio2** and **radio3**, among many others. Notice that URLs always use forward slashes rather than the back-slashes used for paths in Windows.
index.html	This is the name of the file we're opening. The .html (or .htm) extension indicates that it's a Web page, but browsers can handle many different types of file.

+info

URLs without filenames

Sometimes you'll come across a URL that ends with a directory name, such as http://www.bbc.co.uk/radio1/ *or* http://www.bbc.co.uk/radio1 *(the final slash is optional). When a browser sends this URL to a Web server, the server looks in that directory for a* default *file, often called* **index.htm** *or* **index.html.** *If a file with this name is found, it's sent back to the browser. If not, the server may send back a rather dull-looking list of the files in that directory, or (more often these days) it may send an even duller-looking 'file not found' message.*

Once you know how URLs work, hypertext links are easy to understand. When you write a Web page and want to include a link to another file, you type two things into the page: the first is the URL of the file to link to, and the second is the text that visitors to the page will be able to see and click on. There's a little more to it than that, but not much.

When your browser displays this page, it recognises that what you typed is a link and treats it differently from ordinary text. Initially it displays the text in a different colour and underlines it. If the mouse moves over the text, the usual mouse pointer turns into a hand shape and the URL of the linked page is shown in the status bar at the bottom of the browser window. If you click this text, the browser tries to fetch the appropriate page from the Web server on which it's stored, and (if all goes well) that Web server sends the file back for your browser to display.

HTML – the language of the Web

A moment ago I explained very briefly how a hypertext link was added to a Web page, and said there was a little more to it. Here we are at the 'little more' – a language called **HTML** (HyperText Markup Language).

So what's HTML all about? Well, we've met **hypertext** already – the clickable links that are used to navigate from one Web page to another. A **markup language** is a set of codes or symbols added to plain text to indicate how it should be presented to the reader, noting bold or italic text, typefaces to be used, paragraph breaks, and so on. When you type text into your word processor, it adds those codes for you but tactfully hides them from view: if you wanted bold text, for example, it shows you bold text instead of those codes. In HTML, however, you have to type those codes along with the text, and your browser puts the whole lot together before displaying it.

These codes are known as tags, and they consist of ordinary text placed between less-than (<) and greater-than (>) signs. Let's take an example:

```
<B>Welcome to my home page!</B> Thank you for
visiting.
```

The first tag, `<B>`, means 'turn on bold type'. Halfway through the line the same tag is used again, but with a forward slash inserted straight after the less-than sign: this means 'turn off bold type'. If you displayed a page containing this line in your browser it would look like this:

```
Welcome to my home page! Thank you for visiting.
```

Of course, there's more to a Web page than bold text, so clearly there must be many more of these tags. Don't let that put you off – over the coming chapters I'll introduce a few at a time, and you don't have to learn them all! There's a little bundle that you'll use a lot, and you'll get to know those very quickly. Others will begin to sink in once you've used them a few times.

Do I need special software?

Believe it or not, creating a Web site is something you really can do for free (once you've bought a computer, that is). Because HTML is entirely text-based, you can write your pages in a simple text editor such as Windows' Notepad accessory, and throughout this book I'm going to assume that's what you're doing (Fig. 1.2). There are better text editors around that will let you keep several documents open at once and switch between them, and many of those are free to download from shareware sites such as http://tucows.mirror.ac.uk and http://www.shareware.com. Indeed, you can use any other word processor you want to, but you'll have to remember to save your files as

Figure 1.2

A Web page in Notepad – no expensive software needed!

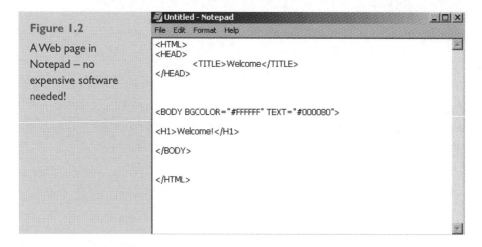

```
Untitled - Notepad
File  Edit  Format  Help

<HTML>
<HEAD>
          <TITLE>Welcome</TITLE>
</HEAD>


<BODY BGCOLOR="#FFFFFF" TEXT="#000080">

<H1>Welcome!</H1>

</BODY>


</HTML>
```

plain text when you've finished. But there are other options, so let's quickly run through them.

WYSIWYG editors

In theory, WYSIWYG editors are the perfect tools for designing Web pages and sites: instead of looking at plain text with HTML tags dotted around it, you see your Web page itself gradually taking shape, with images, colours and formatting all displayed. It's a lot like working with desktop publishing (DTP) software, and most DTP applications now offer the option of saving your results as a Web page. Another benefit is that WYSIWYG editors come with a set of preset templates and pre-defined styles or themes: you can sort through the templates to find the right look and feel for your site, and then simply 'fill in the blanks' to add your own content and change the captions on buttons and banner-headings.

Maybe now you're thinking: 'Yippee! I don't have to learn all that HTML stuff!' Unfortunately that's not quite the case. Once in a while, for instance, the editor won't do what you want it to do, so you'll have to switch to its text-editing mode and juggle the HTML tags yourself. And what if you see something clever on someone else's page and want to find out how it was done? If you don't know the language, you might remain envious forever! That said, if you'd like to give the WYSIWYG method a shot, here are some of the most popular applications:

+info

WYSIWYG
A delightful acronym (pronounced 'wizzywig') for 'What you see is what you get'. This is used to describe many different types of software that can show you on the screen exactly what something will look like when you print it on paper or view it in your Web browser.

Find out how someone else's page was put together
In Internet Explorer, right-click on the page and choose **View Source** to see the HTML code in Notepad. In Netscape, right-click and choose **View Frame Source**. You can also choose a similar option from either browser's **View** menu.

- **Macromedia Dreamweaver** from http://www.macromedia.com

- **Adobe GoLive** from http://www.adobe.com

- **NetObjects Fusion** from http://www.netobjects.com (Fig. 1.3)

Figure 1.3

Building a page from a
template in NetObjects
Fusion.

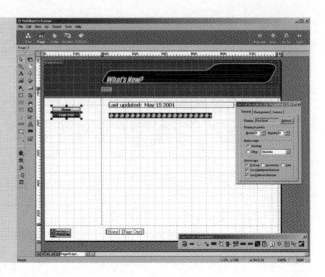

HTML markup editors

Using a markup editor is rather like using Notepad – you see all the
HTML code on the page in front of you. But instead of having to type
all the tags yourself, a markup editor will insert them for you at the
click of a button or the press of a hotkey, in the same way that you use
your word processor. For example, if a piece of text should be in bold
type, you click the **Bold** button on the toolbar (or press **Ctrl+B**) and
then type the text in the usual way. This makes for a speedier way of
working, and helps you avoid typing mistakes in the tags.

Markup editors are also ideal for newcomers to HTML. If you
don't know one tag from another, just click the appropriate buttons
on the toolbar to insert them: once you've seen them appear on the
page a few times, you'll soon start to remember what's what! Here
are three of the most popular and feature-packed markup editors:

● **HomeSite** from http://www.allaire.com (Fig. 1.4)

● **HTMLed** from http://www.ist.ca

● **HoTMetaL Pro** from http://www.sq.com

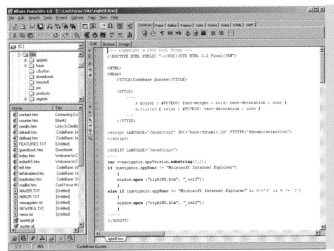

Figure 1.4
Handy colour-coding and one-click tag insertion in HomeSite.

Expanding your browser collection

There are three Web browsers in common use: Microsoft Internet Explorer (the most popular browser by a huge margin), Netscape and Opera. Although all three are very similar, there can be slight differences in the way each displays a particular Web page. More importantly, if you make a mistake in your HTML coding it may make no difference at all in one browser and a huge difference in another!

While you're designing your site, you need at least one browser so that you can look at the result – it doesn't really matter which of those you choose, though I'd recommend Internet Explorer as it's the most widely used of the three. Before you actually publish your site on the Web, though, it's important to check it in all the popular browsers to make sure

> **Ugh, that's horrible!**
> *While you're planning your site, consider what you like (and especially what you dislike) about other sites you've visited, and avoid committing the same crimes yourself. It's easy to start adding things simply because you can and forget how irritating they are. Background music that can't be turned off, garish background images that make the text difficult to read, links that don't give any clue about what they're linking to – a quick critical look at a few Web sites from a user's point of view will teach you a lot as a designer.*

there are no problems. Fortunately, all three are free, so you can just visit their Web sites to download them:

- Microsoft Internet Explorer at http://www.microsoft.com/windows/ie or http://www.microsoft.com/mac/ie
- Netscape at http://home.netscape.com/download
- Opera at http://www.operasoftware.com

2

A simple Web page

- **Organise your folders and create a basic Web page template**
- **Choose a title, and add a heading and text to the page**
- **Apply bold or italic effects to text**
- **Learn how to align headings and paragraphs**
- **Get to grips with tag attributes**

Every great Web site starts with a single page, and in this chapter we'll get that first page under way. To keep things simple, we're just going to deal with the text elements of a page to begin with, using headings and paragraphs, alignment, and useful text effects such as bold and italic. In later chapters we'll look at ways of making everything more attractive with images, colours and layout options, and we'll link pages together to create a mini Web site. As you work through these chapters, try creating the same example pages yourself and experimenting with some of the tags to see what happens. Remember, you can't break anything by doing it wrong, so it pays to be adventurous!

Getting organised

First, we need to sort out where all the files that will eventually make up your Web site are going to be kept: if they're scattered around your hard disk in different places you'll have to remember the names and locations of all those files later on, and that won't be much fun! Make a new folder somewhere on your hard disk, and call it **Site** (or something more imaginative but equally recognisable). Open this new folder, and create another inside it called **images**. (I do recommend using that name for it: this is where all the image files used on your site will be kept, so the name will be easy to remember and understand in future. We'll return to this in Chapters 4 and 5.)

This leads to two important points about the naming of files and folders (or **directories**, as folders are known on the Internet):

1 Names are case-sensitive, so if your site includes a link to **MyPicture.jpg**, but you actually called the file **mypicture.jpg**, the image won't be displayed. For this reason, it's simplest to name all files and directories using *entirely lower-case names*, removing that potential hazard.

2 The names of files and directories mustn't include spaces. This is a basic rule that applies to any Internet address, including email addresses. The names can be as long as you like, and you can use hyphens, underscores or dots to separate individual words in the names if you really can't bear the idea of having files named **whatsnew.htm** or **productsandservices.htm**.

Throughout the book, I'll refer to your 'Site directory' and your 'images directory', meaning the two directories you've just created, whatever you've chosen to call them.

Making a template file

There are a few bits and pieces that will appear in almost every Web page you write, so let's begin by making a template file that you can use every time you start work on a new page. Start Notepad, or whichever text editor you're using, and type the text below. Don't worry about the exact number of spaces, tabs or carriage returns you type.

```
<HTML>
<HEAD>
        <TITLE>Untitled</TITLE>
</HEAD>
<BODY>


</BODY>
</HTML>
```

Save this file in your Site directory, giving it the name **template.htm** or **template.html.** When saving from Notepad, make sure you type the .htm or .html extension after the name as well: if you just type **template** as the filename, Notepad will save the file as **template.txt**.

As I mentioned in Chapter 1, the pieces of text between the < and > signs are known as **tags** and they tell the browser how to display the page. None of the tags in this template page does anything exciting by itself, but it's worth knowing what they're for. The entire page is placed between <HTML> and </HTML> tags, and it's divided into two separate chunks: the **head** (the section between the <HEAD> and </HEAD> tags) and the **body**

> **+info**
>
> Should I use .htm or .html?
> It doesn't matter whether you use .htm or .html as the file extension for your pages, since all browsers recognise either of those as being Web pages. However, you'll find life a lot easier if you make a decision now and stick to the same extension for every page you save!

(between <BODY> and </BODY>). You'll notice that these tags are used in pairs. The first instance is the *opening* tag, and the second (which is the same, but has a forward slash after the < symbol) is the *closing* tag. Tags that work in pairs like this could be thought of as on/off switches marking the beginning and end of a section, or the start and finish of an ongoing effect to be applied to their contents. (A good example of this is the tag for bold text I mentioned on page 5.)

The **head** section is pretty dull: all it contains is the title of the page, inserted between the <TITLE> and </TITLE> tags. There are other bits and pieces that can be slotted in here, but the title is the only element that *must* be there.

The **body** section is the one that matters. Between these two tags you'll type all the text that should appear on the page, and put in the tags needed to display images, set colours, insert hyperlinks to other pages and sites, and anything else you want your page to contain.

Now that we've created and saved a basic template file, let's start adding to it to build up a respectable-looking page. In your Site directory, make a copy of the file (so that you keep this template file unchanged for creating more pages from later). Rename the copy to **index.htm** or **index.html,** and open it in Notepad.

Capital letters

When you type tags, you can use upper-case or lower-case letters. If you prefer <title>, or <Title>, or even <tItLe>, it's all the same to a browser. But typing tags in capitals makes them stand out from the ordinary text on the page, which can be useful when editing a page, and it tends to be simpler to do when you've got to use the Shift key to type the < and > symbols anyway.

Adding a title, heading and text

Choose your title carefully!

For a couple of reasons, the title of the page is more important than it might seem. First, most search engines will list the title of your page in their search results (see Chapter 9), so it needs to be interesting enough to make people want to visit it. Second, if someone likes your page enough to add it to their Favorites or Bookmarks list, this is the title they'll see in the list when they open it.

The first thing to do is to replace the word **Untitled** with a sensible title for the page, such as **A1 Graphic Design Company** or **My EastEnders HomePage**. Pick something that describes what the page will be about, but keep it fairly short: the text between the <TITLE> and </TITLE> tags will appear in the title bar at the very top of most browsers, and if your entry is too long to fit, it'll just get chopped off!

Now we'll add some text to the page. To keep things simple, type what I've entered below. When you've done that, save the file, but don't close Notepad yet.

```
<HTML>
<HEAD>
        <TITLE>The Computing Site Directory</TITLE>
</HEAD>
<BODY>
<H1>The Computing Site Directory</H1>
Here's an example first paragraph.

<P>And here's a second paragraph.
</BODY>
</HTML>
```

Now take a look at your masterpiece in a browser. There are several ways you can do that: one is to go to your Site directory and double-click the **index.htm** file so that your default browser starts and displays it; another is to start your browser and use the **Open** option on its File menu to browse for the file. Simpler still, just drag the file's icon from your Site directory and drop it on to the browser window. When your browser opens the page, it should look like Fig. 2.1.

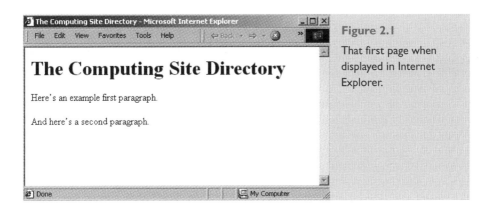

Figure 2.1

That first page when displayed in Internet Explorer.

So what are those new tags all about? Let's take the `<P>` tag first. This tells your browser to present the text that follows as a new paragraph, which automatically inserts a blank line before it. And this raises an important point about HTML: you can't insert blank lines just by pressing **Enter** or **Return** on the keyboard. Although you can see blank lines in Notepad when you do that, a browser will ignore them, which is why you have to start a new paragraph by entering `<P>`. So why did I leave a blank line between the two 'paragraphs' in the HTML code above? Simply because it makes the code easier to read: if blank lines in the code are going to be ignored by the browser, you can sprinkle them around liberally to make the code easier to understand at a glance. I could have written the code this way and the result would have been the same in the browser:

```
Here's an example first paragraph.<P>And here's a
second paragraph.
```

Notice that, unlike the few other tags we've come across so far, there's no `</P>` tag needed: the act of starting a new paragraph isn't an ongoing effect that has to be switched off again later.

The other tags that cropped up were `<H1>` and `</H1>`, which format a line of text as a heading. You can choose from six sizes: `<H1>` is the largest, followed by `<H2>` and `</H2>`, and so on down to the smallest, `<H6>` and `</H6>`. In one nifty little manoeuvre these tags change the size of the text placed between them and make it bold. They also start a new paragraph for the heading automatically (so you don't need a `<P>` tag at the start of the line) and start a new paragraph for whatever follows the heading.

Try experimenting with the different heading sizes by altering the `<H1>` and `</H1>` tags. After each change, resave the file and click your browser's **Refresh** button to make it load and display the new copy of the page.

+info

Start a new line without starting a new paragraph

Another tag, `<BR>`, will give you a 'line break'. In other words, the text that follows the `<BR>` tag will start at the beginning of the next line with no empty line inserted before it. As an example, you could type a list of items, with a `<BR>` tag after each to place it on a separate line (more on that in Chapter 3).

Font formatting

If you've got the idea of the heading tags, you can see that HTML certainly isn't rocket science. Heading tags are easy to use, but not unusually so: there's a bundle of formatting tags that work in exactly the same way – you type the opening tag, some text, and the closing tag. Let's run through some of those now as a quick and painless way to expand your HTML vocabulary.

The tags for bold and italic text are especially easy to remember: `<B>` for bold, and `<I>` for italic, with the appropriate closing tag (`</B>` or `</I>`) when you want the effect to stop. And, just as in your word processor, you can combine these tags to produce combined effects, so if your document contained this:

```
This is <I>italic</I>. This is <B>bold</B>. This is
<B><I>bold and italic</I></B>.
```

the result would look like this in a browser:

This is *italic*. This is **bold**. This is ***bold and italic***.

You could also use those tags like this:

```
<B>This is <I>bold and italic</I>. This is bold but
no longer italic.</B>
```

which a browser would display like this:

This is *bold and italic*. This is bold but no longer italic.

If you really feel the urge, you can underline text using another memorable pair of tags, `<U>` and `</U>`, but be careful how you use underlining: most people surfing the Web expect underlined text to be a hyperlink, so they might find your gratuitous use of these tags confusing.

+info

Putting your tags in order
It doesn't really matter which order the tags appear in. As long as you 'switch off' any ongoing effects before the next piece of text, you'll get the result you wanted. However, it's good coding practice to work on a 'last on, first off' basis, as in `<B><I>Some Text Here</I></B>`.

Adding information with attributes

All the tags we've seen so far are easy to understand and use: they're either self-contained tags like `<P>` and `<BR>` that you slot in to create paragraph or line breaks, or pairs of tags that work as on/off switches, like `<B>` and `</B>`. However, there are other tags that need to contain a little more information about what you want to do. A good example is the `<FONT>` tag, which we'll look at more closely in Chapter 4. By itself it isn't saying anything useful: which font? what size? what colour? You provide this extra information by adding **attributes** to the tag such as `SIZE=3`, `FACE=Arial`, and so on, so a complete font tag might look like this:

```
<FONT SIZE=3 FACE=Arial>
```

Attributes are additional pieces of information slotted into a tag. The name of the tag always comes first (the word `FONT` in the font tag, for example), and the attributes follow the name. Each attribute is separated by a space, and needs an equals sign (=) between the attribute itself and the value you want to set for it. It doesn't matter what order the attributes appear in, and you don't need to include a particular attribute if you don't want to change its value from whatever it was previously set to.

We've already met one tag that has an optional attribute – the heading tags `<H1>` to `<H6>`. These can take an `ALIGN` attribute to specify whether the heading is aligned to the left, middle or right of the page, using the values `LEFT`, `CENTER` or `RIGHT`. In our example page we didn't include this attribute for the heading tag, so we got the default result: a left-aligned heading. We'd have got exactly the same result if we'd used this instead:

```
<H1 ALIGN=LEFT>The Computing Site Directory</H1>
```

Clearly there's no point in bloating our Web page with extra code that won't do anything useful, but try replacing that line with either:

```
<H1 ALIGN=CENTER>The Computing Site Directory</H1>
```

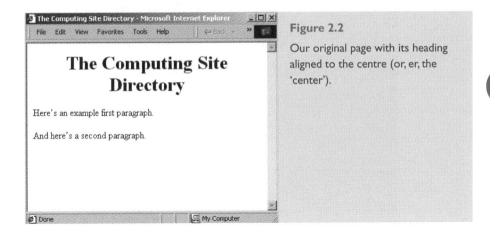

The Computing Site Directory

Here's an example first paragraph.

And here's a second paragraph.

Done   My Computer

Figure 2.2

Our original page with its heading aligned to the centre (or, er, the 'center').

or

```
<H1 ALIGN=RIGHT>The Computing Site Directory</H1>
```

As usual, save the edited page and refresh your browser to see the result. In Fig. 2.2 I've aligned the heading to the centre of the page. Because the window is a little smaller, the browser has wrapped the heading on to a second line: this is handled automatically for all headings and paragraphs. (Of course, if I wanted the heading always to be split over two lines, I could insert a `<BR>` tag before the word 'Directory'.)

> *Watch your spelling!*
> *HTML is an American language, so watch out for those little differences in spelling such as **color** instead of colour, and **center** instead of centre. If you spell the name of a tag or attribute wrongly, the browser won't try to make sense of it, it'll just ignore it.*

Aligning paragraphs

If you can choose how a heading should be aligned on the page, surely you can do the same thing with a paragraph of ordinary text? Yes you can, and the `<P>` tag comes to the rescue here in much the same way that the heading tag did earlier: by offering an ALIGN attribute with one of the following values after its = sign:

Value	Meaning
LEFT	Aligns the paragraph to the left of the page
CENTER	Centres the paragraph on the page
RIGHT	Aligns the paragraph to the right of the page
JUSTIFY	Justifies the paragraph (to give a straight edge to the left and right of the page, achieved by adding extra space between words). This is a recent addition to HTML that only the latest browsers understand: older browsers will ignore it and use the default value (LEFT).

At the moment our example page just contains a couple of short dummy paragraphs – not enough to do any serious paragraph formatting with – so let's replace those with something more meaningful so that the page looks like this:

```
<HTML>
<HEAD>
     <TITLE>The Computing Site Directory</TITLE>
</HEAD>
<BODY>
<H1 ALIGN=CENTER>The Computing Site Directory</H1>

<P>Welcome to the Computing Site Directory, the
number one resource for all your computing needs:
industry news and comment, freeware and shareware
software, magazines and journals, hardware driver
updates, and much more.

<P>Select a category below to choose from a
frequently-updated list of the best sites available.
If any link is broken, please contact the Webmaster.
</BODY>
</HTML>
```

If you were to look at the page in your browser now, you'd see that both paragraphs are aligned to the left: the `<P>` tags don't include the `ALIGN` attribute, so we're getting the default alignment. In fact, apart from replacing the text to be displayed, the only change I've made is to add a `<P>` tag before the *first* paragraph as well as the second. At the moment that first `<P>` tag is being ignored: the heading automatically created a paragraph break for us, so we've got the equivalent of two `<P>` tags in a row before the first paragraph. HTML

> **More white space needed!**
> *If you want to create a block of white space on the page, you can't use several `<P>` tags in a row to do it. But after a `<P>` tag (or instead of one) you can type as many `<BR>` tags as you like. Unlike the `<P>` tag, these are cumulative.*

doesn't allow paragraphs to be blank, so one of these is disregarded. (We could type `<P><P><P><P><P>` and all but one of those would be ignored!)

Now alter those paragraphs again to look like the following (the changes are shown in bold type) and view the result in your browser.

```
<P ALIGN=CENTER>Welcome to the Computing Site
Directory, the number one resource for all your
computing needs: industry news and comment, free-
ware and shareware software, magazines and
journals, hardware driver updates, and much
more.</P>

<P ALIGN=CENTER>Select a category below to choose
from a frequently-updated list of the best sites
available. If any link is broken, please contact
the Webmaster.</P>
```

We've made the same two changes to both paragraphs. First, we've centred the paragraphs by adding the `ALIGN=CENTER` attribute (Fig. 2.3). Second, we've added a closing `</P>` tag to mark the end of the paragraph. Yes, I know I said earlier that the `<P>` tag was self-contained. I lied. But although it *does* have a closing tag, that closing tag is only needed when you use the `ALIGN` attribute: it tells the browser where to stop applying the alignment. If you didn't

Figure 2.3

Adding `<P ALIGN= CENTER>` to both paragraphs.

include the closing `</P>` tag, you could find that text further down the page was still being centred or right-aligned.

Centring text

Part of the reason I've used the `<P>` tag to align the paragraphs was to introduce the concept of adding attributes to tags. Most of the time you'll want your paragraphs to be left-aligned, which needs no `ALIGN` attribute and no closing `</P>` tag, and you probably won't want to right-align or justify text very often. That just leaves centred text, and there's a better and more memorable way to do that: the `<CENTER>...</CENTER>` tag pair.

The handy thing about the `<CENTER>` tag is that it can be applied to anything on a page: a heading, a paragraph or an image. Just put the opening tag before the start of the content to be centred and the closing tag where the centring should end. So a less fussy way to centre the heading and the two paragraphs would be this:

```
<HTML>
<HEAD>
        <TITLE>The Computing Site Directory</TITLE>
</HEAD>
<BODY>
<CENTER>
<H1>The Computing Site Directory</H1>
```

```
Welcome to the Computing Site Directory, the number
one resource for all your computing needs: industry
news and comment, freeware and shareware software,
magazines and journals, hardware driver updates,
and much more.

<P>Select a category below to choose from a fre-
quently-updated list of the best sites available.
If any link is broken, please contact the
Webmaster.
</CENTER>
</BODY>
</HTML>
```

We're back to one `<P>` tag, no closing `</P>` tags, and no `ALIGN` attributes! It's a lot easier to understand, and it gives the same result as the more complicated version of the page.

DIV – the easy way to align

Apart from the heading and paragraph tags there are other tags that can take an optional `ALIGN` attribute, such as images and tables (covered later in the book). If your page contains a number of headings, paragraphs, images and/or tables that have to be aligned the same way, that could add up to a lot of `ALIGN` attributes. A better option is to use a single tag, `<DIV>` (short for *division*). This also takes an `ALIGN` attribute, but it works just like the `<CENTER>` tag: everything between the `<DIV>` and `</DIV>` tags will be aligned the same way. In fact, the `<CENTER>` tag is actually just an abbreviated form of `<DIV ALIGN=CENTER>`. If an element somewhere between the opening and closing `<DIV>` tags needs to be aligned differently, just add the `ALIGN` attribute to its tag: individual tags' own `ALIGN` attributes override the `<DIV>` alignment.

The `<DIV>` tag really comes into its own when used with style sheets. Skip ahead to Chapter 8 to find out more.

3

Lists, links and special characters

- **Make simple lists using `<BR>` tags**
- **Create smarter-looking lists with bullets and numbering**
- **Create hypertext links to other Web pages or email addresses**
- **Learn how to link your own site's pages together**
- **Use foreign characters and symbols, and add invisible comments**

 In Chapter 2 we put together a basic Web page incorporating a heading and a couple of paragraphs of text, and got to grips with some HTML formatting tags and their attributes. In this chapter we'll get down to the nitty-gritty – how one page links to another to create a Web site of multiple pages. Along the way we'll look at some more aspects of text formatting such as lists, word breaks and spacing, and how you can display symbols and foreign language characters in a Web page. We'll also cover something that's vital in any programming or markup language: how to add comments and notes to the page for your own reference without mucking up its appearance.

Creating lists

If you've followed Chapter 2 and created the same example Web page I did, your second paragraph refers to a list of categories on the page from which the visitor can choose a section of the site to visit. We'll start by making that list of categories, and later in this chapter we'll convert them to links.

The simplest way to make a list in a Web page is to separate each item by either a `<BR>` or a `<P>` tag (depending on how much space you want between each item). For example, we could insert the following just before the closing `</CENTER>` tag in our Web page, which would give the result shown in Fig. 3.1.

```
<P>Computing News and Reviews
<BR>Free Software
<BR>Shareware Software
<BR>Software Companies
<BR>Hardware Companies
<BR>Magazines and Journals
<BR>Hardware Drivers
```

(Because we've placed this list before the closing `</CENTER>` tag, every item is centred on the page. For a left-aligned list, place the added code *after* the `</CENTER>` tag instead.)

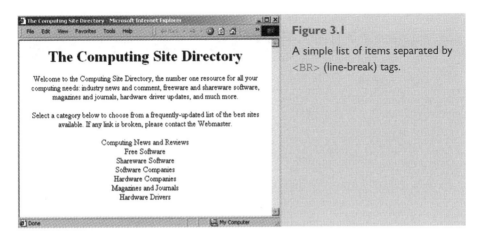

Figure 3.1

A simple list of items separated by `<BR>` (line-break) tags.

The `<P>` tag is used to place a paragraph break between our second paragraph and the beginning of the list. The `<BR>` tags then create a line break before the next item of text. Although this is a perfectly valid way to make a list, and I'm going to stick with it for our example page, HTML includes some easy-to-use tags for creating numbered and bulleted lists, so let's run through those.

Bulleted lists

HTML refers to a bulleted list as an *unordered list* (Fig. 3.2), and uses the tags `<UL>` and `</UL>` to mark the beginning and end of lists. Each item in the list is prefixed with an `<LI>` tag (short for List Item). The `<LI>` tag automatically places each item on a new line, so there's no need to insert line or paragraph breaks. We could make an unordered list of the same items like this:

```
<UL>
<LI>Computing News and Reviews
<LI>Free Software
<LI>Shareware Software
<LI>Software Companies
<LI>Hardware Companies
<LI>Magazines and Journals
<LI>Hardware Drivers
</UL>
```

Figure 3.2

A bulleted (or *unordered*) list.

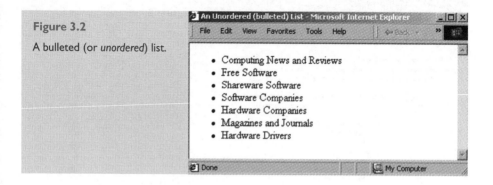

Create a Web site

In Internet Explorer, the type of bullet used is decided for you – you have no control over that. Netscape and Opera add a TYPE attribute to the `<UL>` tag which lets you choose the shape of the bullet:

Attribute	Result
TYPE=DISC	The default bullet, a solid circle
TYPE=CIRCLE	A hollow circular bullet
TYPE=SQUARE	A solid square bullet

Numbered lists

The numbered list is known as an *ordered list*, using the tags `<OL>` and `</OL>`, but it's constructed in the same way as the unordered list above, using the `<LI>` tag for each list item:

```
<OL>
<LI>Computing News and Reviews
<LI>Free Software
<LI>Shareware Software
<LI>Software Companies
<LI>Hardware Companies
<LI>Magazines and Journals
<LI>Hardware Drivers
</OL>
```

+info

Using TYPE=SQUARE *in Internet Explorer*
If you use the TYPE *attribute and your page is viewed in Internet Explorer, it won't cause any problems. Internet Explorer (and any other browser) will always ignore any attributes they don't understand, so your list will still be displayed properly but in the default bullet style.*

The code above would create a list that looked like this:

1 Computing News and Reviews

2 Free Software

3 Shareware Software

4 Software Companies

5 Hardware Companies

6 Magazines and Journals

7 Hardware Drivers

In an ordered list, there's another attribute, `TYPE`, that can be added to the `<OL>` tag, and this is supported by all three popular browsers. The `TYPE` attribute sets the numbering system to be used:

Attribute	Result
TYPE=1	The default numbering system: 1, 2, 3...
TYPE=i	Small roman numerals: i, ii, iii...
TYPE=I	Large roman numerals: I, II, III...
TYPE=A	Upper-case letters: A, B, C...
TYPE=a	Lower-case letters: a, b, c...

Linking to other sites

> **Using quote symbols for attributes**
> To do things by the book, the value of any attribute should really be enclosed between double quotes: `ALIGN="LEFT"`, `TYPE="DISC"`, and so on. In practice, though, the only time quotes are actually needed is when the value contains a space or any punctuation that may make it unclear where the value ends (in URLs, for example). The simple rule is: if in doubt, use quotes – it won't do any harm.

Before we start adding more pages to our example site and linking them together, let's take a quick detour and find out how to create links to *other* Web sites. In HTML, links are known as **anchors**, and they use the `<A>...</A>` tag pair. This is a tag that does nothing at all without attributes, and the attribute we need is `HREF` (short for *Hypertext REFerence*) to specify the URL of the site we're linking to. Between the opening and closing anchor tags goes the text that visitors can click on to visit that site. Here's an example that links to Microsoft's Web site:

```
<A HREF="http://www.microsoft.com">Click here to
visit Microsoft's site.</A>
```

Figure 3.3

A hypertext link to www.microsoft.com.

If you added that line of code to the body of a Web page, the result would look like Fig. 3.3. As you can see, the text is automatically underlined, a hand-cursor appears when the mouse moves over it, and the URL it links to is shown in the browser's status bar. What's more, it works! If you click it, you'll arrive at the URL you typed into the HREF attribute.

Although we just placed one short line of text between the <A> and </A> tags, we could have used something much longer – several paragraphs, for example. You can use other tags within the linking text as well, perhaps to make the link bold or italic, or format it as a heading, so the code below is perfectly valid (although perhaps not altogether practical!), making everything on the page act as a link to Microsoft's site.

```
<BODY>
<CENTER>
<A HREF="http://www.microsoft.com">
<H1>The Computing Site Directory</H1>
Here's an example first paragraph.

<P>And here's a second paragraph.
</A>
</CENTER>
</BODY>
</HTML>
```

Linking to particular pages or files

The link we used in the examples above was to the URL http://www.microsoft.com. We haven't specified a filename, so if this link were clicked Microsoft's server would send back the default Web page from the root directory of this site – in other words, the first page of the Microsoft Web site. If we'd wanted to link to a particular page on that site, we could have entered the complete URL of that page – perhaps something like http://www.microsoft.com/uk/preview/default.htm.

Links don't necessarily have to point to Web pages, though. You can create a link to an image file, a sound or movie file, a zip archive, or any other type of file – the anchor tag is constructed in exactly the same way and only the URL has to change. If the user's browser is capable of displaying the file, it will. Otherwise, the user will be offered the choice of downloading and saving the file on their hard disk or choosing a program on their hard disk that is able to display or play the file.

Creating email links

An email link looks like any other link on the page, but when a visitor clicks it their email program will start and they can send a message to the email address included in the anchor tag. That email address is automatically added to the To field of the message, so all they need to do is type the message and click the **Send** button.

Email links use the same `<A>...</A>` tag as other links, with the URL replaced by an email address. The only other difference is that the email address is prefixed with **mailto:**. We can make use of this in our example Web page. At the moment, our second paragraph ends with the words *If any link is broken, please contact the Webmaster.* Let's encourage user feedback by making the last few words an email link: just replace that sentence with the following, replacing my email address with your own:

```
If any link is broken, please <A HREF="mailto:
rob@codebase.co.uk">contact the Webmaster</A>.
```

Figure 3.4
Our example Web page
with an added email link,
shown in Opera.

If you've followed the changes we've made to our example page, it should look like Fig. 3.4.

Linking to pages on your own site

The links we created to Microsoft's Web site a few pages back used something called an **absolute URL**. That's probably the only type of URL you've come across so far: an absolute URL gives the whole path to the page or file you want to link to, including the http:// prefix and the name of the computer (such as www.microsoft.com). When you want to create links to pages on your own site, you can use a simpler method.

To demonstrate this, of course, we're going to need a second page to link to! Make a copy of the template file you created in Chapter 2 and call it **news.htm**. (Apart from the template file, your Site directory should now contain index.htm and news.htm.)

Open news.htm in your editor and alter it to look like this:

```
<HTML>
<HEAD>
        <TITLE>Computing News and Reviews</TITLE>
```

```
</HEAD>
<BODY>
<CENTER>
<H1>Computing News and Reviews</H1>
</CENTER>
</BODY>
</HTML>
```

Save the changes and reopen index.htm in the editor. At the beginning of our list of categories we've got a *Computing News and Reviews* item, so let's make it into a link to the news.htm page by enclosing it in an anchor tag:

```
<P><A HREF="news.htm">Computing News and Reviews</A>
```

Yes, it's just a filename. This is called a **relative URL** – it tells the browser to look for a file called news.htm and display it. Since the browser doesn't know where else to look, it searches the directory containing the document it's displaying at the moment. As long as news.htm really is in the same directory, the browser will find and open it when the link is clicked (Fig. 3.5). You can test this by saving the index.htm file and refreshing the browser in the usual way, then clicking this new link. (If a file with that name *isn't* in that directory, the browser will display the all-too-familiar 'not found' message instead.)

You can also make a browser look somewhere different for a file in a similar way. Go to your Site directory and create a new directory inside it called **pages**. Move the news.htm file into this new directory. If you click the link we just created, it will now fail because the browser can't find the file: we need to change the link to the following:

+info

Relative URLs

What's so great about relative URLs? First, less typing, which also minimises the opportunities to make mistakes. More importantly, though, you can test these links in your browser while you're designing your site to check that they work. If you used an absolute URL such as http://www.mysite.com/mypage.htm, *your browser would have to connect to the Internet, find www.mysite.com and retrieve mypage.htm from it. That's time-consuming, and it would only work if you'd actually uploaded mypage.htm to the server.*

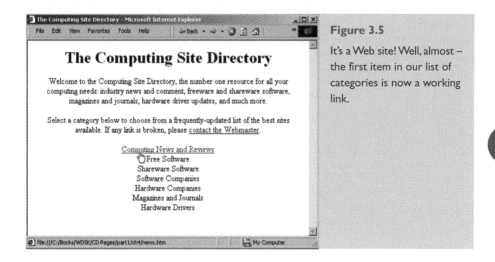

Figure 3.5

It's a Web site! Well, almost – the first item in our list of categories is now a working link.

```
<P><A  HREF="pages/news.htm">Computing  News  and
Reviews</A>
```

This tells the browser to look in the current directory for another directory named **pages**, and search inside that for a file named news.htm. If you test this in your browser, the news.htm page should once again be found and opened. (For another example, you could create a new directory inside 'pages' called 'morepages' and move news.htm into that. The link would then need to be: `<A HREF="pages/morepages/news.htm">`. For the purposes of our example site, we'll leave news.htm in the 'pages' directory.)

What we're lacking now is a link back to our index.htm page from news.htm. If news.htm were still in the Site directory, we'd use `<A HREF="index.htm">` but it's now in a subdirectory called 'pages', so we need to tell the browser to look in the *parent* directory of 'pages' to find the file. If you're familiar with MS-DOS, you'll recognise this straight away: to move up one level in the directory tree, you type two dots followed by a forward slash. So we can add the following line to the news.htm page, after the heading:

```
<A HREF="../index.htm">Home</A>
```

And if news.htm were in that 'morepages' directory, the anchor tag to get back to the index page would be `<A HREF="../../index.htm">Home</A>`.

What next?

If you're treating this as a tutorial and building the same site, follow the same steps for the remaining six items in the category list on the index page. Make six copies of news.htm inside the 'pages' directory, give the files appropriate names, and edit their `<TITLE>` and `<H1>` tags to correspond to the six categories. You can then add the appropriate anchor tags to those six list items so that the list looks something like this:

```
<P><A   HREF="pages/news.htm">Computing   News   and
Reviews</A>
<BR><A HREF="pages/free.htm">Free Software</A>
<BR><A HREF="pages/shareware.htm">Shareware Software
</A>
<BR><A HREF="pages/softcomp.htm">Software Companies
</A>
<BR><A HREF="pages/hardcomp.htm">Hardware Companies
</A>
<BR><A HREF="pages/mags.htm">Magazines and Journals
</A>
<BR><A HREF="pages/drivers.htm">Hardware Drivers</A>
```

Voilà! You now have a fully linked (if rather dull!) Web site consisting of eight pages.

Spaces and word breaks

Now that you've worked with HTML for a while, you may have come across this phenomenon: you type two or three spaces into the code, but the browser insists on using just one. This is supposed to happen. Just as browsers ignore your use of the Enter or Return key in your code, they also ignore the Tab key and cut multiple spaces down to one.

You can get around this by using one of a set of special character codes,   (short for *non-breaking space*). This code must be in lower-case, and placed between an ampersand and a semi-colon. To insert three spaces in a row, then, you'd enter   .

Special characters

There are several other characters that browsers can't display when typed into a page in the usual way. These are known as reserved characters: they form a part of the HTML language so they have a special meaning to a browser. Like the non-breaking space, there are codes you can use if you need to display these characters in a Web page:

> **Preventing breaks between words**
> Where the line breaks in your paragraphs will occur depends upon the font being used, the size of the user's browser window, and many other variables that you have no control over. If you have a few words in a paragraph that must appear together on the same line, don't use the   code between each word: enclose the words between <NOBR>...</NOBR> (no-break) tags instead.

Character	HTML Code	Numeric Code
< (less than)	&lt;	&#60;
> (greater than)	&gt;	&#62;
" (quote)	&quot;	&#34;
& (ampersand)	&amp;	&#38;
© (copyright)	&copy;	&#169;
™ (trademark)	&trade;	&#153;
¼ (quarter)	&frac14;	&#188;
½ (half)	&frac12;	&#189;
¾ (three-quarters)	&frac34;	&#190;
£ (pound)	&pound;	&#163;
° (degrees)	&deg;	&#176;
× (multiply)	&times;	&#215;
÷ (divide)	&divide;	&#247;

You can use either the HTML code or the numeric code, so to display the text **"Give & Take"** you'd type either of the following:

```
&#34;Give &#38; Take&#34;
&quot;Give &amp; Take&quot;
```

Yes, it looks untidy, but browsers understand it!

Commenting HTML code

Whatever language you're programming or coding in, it's useful to be able to add your own notes or **comments** to the code that will be ignored when the code is compiled, run, or (in the case of Web pages) displayed in a browser. You may want to mark particular sections of code to make them easier to find during editing, add reminders about what a section of code does, or make a note of items you want to add later. HTML has its own comment tag pair, `<!--` and `-->`, just for this purpose. Anything enclosed between these tags will be ignored by the browser when the page is displayed.

Another handy use for these tags is to *comment out* sections of HTML code: you can effectively remove chunks of text or HTML code from the page by enclosing them between comment tags rather than deleting them. In the code below, for example, only the first two items in the list would be displayed on the page. The remaining five are enclosed between comment tags, making them invisible to the browser.

```
<P><A  HREF="pages/news.htm">Computing  News  and
Reviews</A>
<BR><A HREF="pages/free.htm">Free Software</A>
<!--<BR><A    HREF="pages/shareware.htm">Shareware
Software</A>
<BR><A HREF="pages/softcomp.htm">Software Companies
</A>
<BR><A HREF="pages/hardcomp.htm">Hardware Companies
</A>
<BR><A HREF="pages/mags.htm">Magazines  and  Journals
</A>
<BR><A  HREF="pages/drivers.htm">Hardware  Drivers
</A>-->
```

4

Colours, fonts and rules

- Choose colours for the background, text and links
- Add a tiled background image to the page
- Pick fonts, and change the font type or colour for particular items of text
- Use horizontal rules to divide up a Web page

At this stage you're the proud owner of a basic Web site consisting of several pages (although only the index page contains anything useful so far). As it stands, it won't win any awards, but what matters most is that you've worked with HTML tags and their attributes and seen the effect they have on plain text when the result is viewed in a browser. Armed with this experience, let's improve the look of the site by adding colours, choosing fonts, and applying more design touches.

You too can have a <BODY> like mine!

Even in our most impressive page, **index.htm**, everything still looks a bit dull. The background is white, the text is black, the hyperlinks are either blue or purple (depending upon whether you've clicked them or not) – these are the default colours set up by most browsers, and they use those colours because we haven't told them to use anything different. All this is easily changed, though, by adding attributes to the `<BODY>` tag.

I mentioned at the beginning of Chapter 2 that the `<BODY>` tag and its closing `</BODY>` tag must be included in every page, and that's true: they tell the browser where the displayable part of the page begins and ends. The `<BODY>` tag's attributes are all optional, but for any attribute that's missing a browser will use its own default setting, and different browsers may have different defaults. Since most Web authors like to keep as much control as possible over how their pages will be displayed, they add these attributes. There's quite a number of possible attributes, but for the moment we're concerned with colour, which brings the total down to five:

This attribute...	...has this effect
BGCOLOR	Sets the background colour of the page
TEXT	Sets the colour of ordinary text on the page
LINK	Sets the colour of a hyperlink
VLINK	Sets the colour of a link to a previously visited page
ALINK	Sets the colour of an 'active' link (the time between the link being clicked and the new page opening)

Open index.htm in your editor and change its `<BODY>` tag so that it looks like this:

```
<BODY BGCOLOR=MAROON TEXT=WHITE LINK=YELLOW VLINK=
OLIVE ALINK=LIME>
```

Save the page and view the result in your browser (Fig. 4.1). Okay, the colour scheme may not be to your taste (in fact, I hope it isn't!), but you can clearly see the difference made by adding colour attributes to the `<BODY>` tag. Try swapping colours around to find a scheme you prefer. There are 140 **named colours** to choose from like those above, and you'll find them listed in Appendix A. If you'd like each page

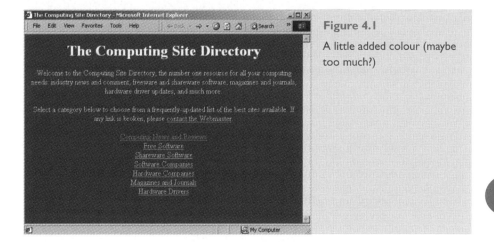

Figure 4.1

A little added colour (maybe too much?)

of your site to use a similar scheme, copy and paste the new `<BODY>` tag into your other pages to replace their empty `<BODY>` tags.

Rather than copying and pasting identical `<BODY>` tags into all your pages to change their colours, you could create a single style sheet to be applied to every page, so that a simple change to the sheet would be reflected throughout your site. Skip ahead to Chapter 8 to learn about style sheets.

Adding a background image

Another attribute you can add to the `<BODY>` tag is `BACKGROUND`. This specifies a GIF or JPEG image file to be used as a background to the Web page, and the image is automatically *tiled* to fill the user's browser window. Because this is a file that the browser has to find, it's entered as a URL just like the `HREF` attribute of the anchor tag (see Chapter 3). And, as with the anchor

+info

Tiled image
When an image is tiled, *multiple copies of the image are placed side by side in rows and columns to fill a specified area. You'd usually want to choose or create an image that can be tiled seamlessly so that the joins between each individual tile are invisible.*

tag, although you could enter an *absolute* URL you'd have to go online to see the result, so a *relative* URL is preferable.

At the beginning of Chapter 2 you created a directory named **images** in your Site directory, and here's your big chance to use it. Find any GIF or JPEG image on your hard disk, or download one from the Web, and copy it into your 'images' directory. You can then add the following attribute to the <BODY> tag of index.htm, changing 'space.jpg' to your own image file's name:

```
BACKGROUND="images/space.jpg"
```

Fig. 4.2 shows the result of using the background image I chose. If I published a page that looked like this, I'd deserve to have my computer taken away: the size of the image is distracting, its repetition is too obvious, and it involves so many colours that the text of the page would be hard to read whatever text colour was used. In Fig. 4.3 I've used something far more subtle: it has a much smaller pattern involving several shades of one colour, and it isn't as eye-catchingly repetitive. A smaller pattern (although it wouldn't reproduce well on the page of this book) would be a better choice still.

Choosing font options

At the moment you're stuck with a single font throughout your site (probably Times New Roman in Windows, and Geneva on a Mac). Like the colour options mentioned at the beginning of this chapter, your browser sets a default font, and different browsers may use different defaults. Fortunately the <FONT>...</FONT> tag pair leaps to your rescue, allowing you to choose and change the font face, size and colour whenever you need to. Here's an example of a <FONT> tag using all three possible attributes:

```
<FONT FACE="Tahoma,Verdana,Arial", SIZE=4 COLOR=red>
```

Figure 4.2

Bad: an appalling choice of background image. Just shoot me.

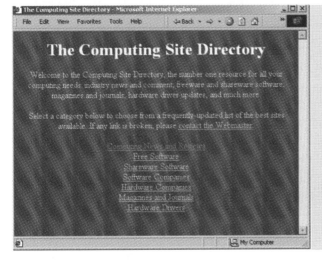

Figure 4.3

Good: the less aware you are of the image, the better.

Let's take these attributes one at a time. The FACE attribute sets the name of the font you want to use, and to prevent errors it's best to always enclose its value in double quotes. Obviously you'd want to choose a font face that's available on your own system so that you can see what it looks like, but the same font needs to be on the system of anyone visiting your site too; if it isn't, their browser will revert to its default font. You can't control what fonts your users have available, of course, and adding the suggestion on your site that visitors should install a particular font will be treated with the indifference it deserves. You can keep a bit of extra control by listing more than one font name (separated by commas) as in the example above. If the first font isn't available, the browser will try for the second, and so on. This way, you can start by specifying the font you'd want used in a perfect world, and work through to something that's at least bearable and likely to be available.

+info

Big text, small text

If you find it hard to keep track of the font size you're currently using, don't bother trying! Instead you can use <BIG> *and* </BIG> *to make the text one step larger than its current setting, or* <SMALL> *and* </SMALL> *to make it one step smaller.*

Font sizes in HTML work differently than in your word processor. There are seven sizes numbered (unsurprisingly) from 1 to 7, where 1 is smallest. The default size for text is 3, so if you wanted to make your text slightly larger, you'd use SIZE=4. The SIZE attribute doesn't affect the headings we covered in Chapter 2, so if there's a heading tag somewhere between your <FONT> and </FONT> tags it will still be formatted in its usual way.

The colour of the text has already been set in the TEXT attribute of the <BODY> tag, covered at the start of this chapter, but you might want to slip in an occasional <FONT COLOR=ivory>...</FONT> to change the colour of a certain word, paragraph or heading. After the closing </FONT> tag, the text colour will revert to the one set in the <BODY> tag.

Choosing fonts

The ability to specify several fonts gives you a lot of flexibility, but you should include at least one font that the majority of users are likely to have available. The increased use of Internet Explorer has been useful in that department: recent versions have included a 'font pack' known as Web Core Fonts which contains Arial, Times New Roman, Georgia, Verdana, Comic Sans MS, Trebuchet MS and Impact, so these fonts will be available on the majority of users' systems (including Macintoshes). The same font pack is included with recent Windows versions, and can be downloaded from http://www.microsoft .com/truetype.

Adding fonts to the index page

Having discovered the <FONT> tag, let's improve the look of our index.htm page by setting a few fonts for it. Alter the code of the page to match the code below (I've marked the changes in bold type) and the result should look similar to Fig. 4.4 when viewed in your browser:

```
<HTML>
<HEAD>
        <TITLE>The Computing Site Directory</TITLE>
</HEAD>
<BODY BGCOLOR=white TEXT=black LINK=blue VLINK=navy
ALINK=red>
<CENTER>
<FONT FACE="Georgia,Times New Roman" SIZE=3>
<FONT FACE="Verdana,Arial"><H1>The Computing Site
Directory</H1></FONT>
Welcome to the <FONT COLOR=maroon>Computing Site
Directory</FONT>, the number one resource for all
your computing needs: industry news and comment,
freeware and shareware software, magazines and
journals, hardware driver updates, and much more.

<P>Select a category below to choose from a fre-
quently-updated list of the best sites available.
If any link is broken, please <A HREF="mailto:rob@
codebase.co.uk?subject=Broken link">contact the
Webmaster</A>.

<P>
<FONT FACE="Verdana,Arial" SIZE=4>
<A HREF="news.htm">Computing News and Reviews</A>
```

Figure 4.4

The index.htm page, with improved colours and the addition of a few <FONT> tags.

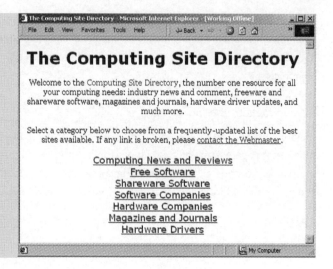

```
<BR><A HREF="free.htm">Free Software</A>
<BR><A HREF="shareware.htm">Shareware Software</A>
<BR><A HREF="softcomp.htm">Software Companies</A>
<BR><A HREF="hardcomp.htm">Hardware Companies</A>
<BR><A HREF="mags.htm">Magazines and Journals</A>
<BR><A HREF="drivers.htm">Hardware Drivers</A>
</FONT>
</CENTER>

</FONT>
</BODY>
</HTML>
```

The first <FONT> tag sets the default font to use for the page; its corresponding </FONT> tag is just above the closing </BODY> tag. This means that everything on the page will be displayed in that font and size unless we specify something different for particular sections. And we've done just that in three places:

● The heading has <FONT> tags enclosing it that specify a different font face. Its size is set by the <H1> tags (we could make it smaller using <H2> or <H3>) and its colour is set in the body tag's TEXT attribute.

- The words 'Computing Site Directory' in the first paragraph have been set to a different colour. Because we haven't included `FACE` or `SIZE` attributes, these remain the same as the other text in that paragraph, set in the very first `<FONT>` tag.

- The list of links has been set a different face and size in a similar way. Adding a `COLOR` attribute here would be ignored: the link colours are set by the `LINK/ALINK/VLINK` attributes of the body tag and can only be changed through the use of style sheets (see Chapter 8).

Page divisions with horizontal rules

Horizontal rules are straight lines with an engraved 3D look that divide a page into sections. For the simplest type of rule, the only tag you need is `<HR>`. This automatically puts a horizontal rule across the full width of the page, placing a paragraph break before and after it. Because the rule isn't an effect that needs to be 'switched off', there's no closing tag.

If you want to, you can change the look of the `<HR>` tag by adding some (or all!) of its available attributes (see table overleaf).

It's worth playing with the `<HR>` tag to find out what you can do with it. For example, the following piece of code places a square bullet in the centre of the page which makes a smart, 'minimalist' divider (Fig. 4.5):

```
<HR WIDTH=10 SIZE=10 NOSHADE COLOR=blue>
```

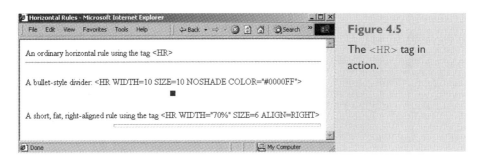

Figure 4.5
The `<HR>` tag in action.

Use this attribute...	...for this result
ALIGN=	Use LEFT or RIGHT to place the rule on one side of the page. Without this attribute the rule will be centred
SIZE=	Enter any number to set the height of the rule in pixels. The default size is two pixels high
WIDTH=	You could enter a number to specify the width of the rule (in pixels), but as you don't know how wide the user's browser window is, this is usually to be avoided. Instead, specify a percentage of the window's width, such as WIDTH="70%"
COLOR=	Enter a colour name to set the colour of the rule. Only Internet Explorer supports this; browsers will ignore it. The default colour varies according to the page's background colour (<BODY BGCOLOR>)
NOSHADE	This removes the 3D shading from the rule leaving a solid line. There's no equals sign and no value to add

5

Getting graphic – images and buttons

- **What you need to create your own Web graphics**
- **Find out how to add images to the page**
- **Place images exactly where you want them**
- **Set the size and spacing of images**
- **Use images as links instead of dull old text**

So far the example site we're building is 'text only' – not a single image in sight. From the point of view of speed, that's not a bad thing: we could work through the seven empty 'category' pages we created, adding links and descriptions for hundreds of great computing sites, and our entire site would probably still weigh in at less than 30 Kb! However, the odds are that you want a more stylish site, and a well-chosen image or two can make a lot of difference to visual impact and layout.

Creating your own images

To create and edit images for use on the Web, you'll need a graphics program capable of working with GIF and JPEG formats (which I'll explain in a moment). These are very common formats, so you may find that the software bundled with your operating system (such as Windows Paint) or your scanner or printer (Adobe PhotoDeluxe, perhaps) will do the job.

Graphics is one area where the quality of the tool can make a lot of difference to the quality of the result, so here are two of the tools used by most professional designers. Although they're both commercial programs, they can be downloaded for a free 30-day trial, so I'd recommend picking one of these and giving it a try.

- **Macromedia Fireworks** from http://www.macromedia.com, an easy to use but comprehensive program aimed at Web graphics creation, with many useful features.

- **Paint Shop Pro** (Fig. 5.1) from http://www.digitalworkshop.co.uk, one of the most popular graphics tools among Web designers, with an animation program included.

The images you use on the Web must be in either **JPEG** or **GIF** format. Unlike some of the other computer graphics formats you can choose from when you save an image, these are *compressed* formats – they save the picture into a much smaller file, and size matters a lot on the Web!

JPEG (pronounced *jay-peg*) stands for Joint Photographic Experts Group and, as the name suggests, it was designed for working with photographs (or more generally, images containing lifelike colouring and shading). JPEG images can contain up to 16.7 million colours.

GIF (pronounced with a hard or a soft 'g' according to taste) is an acronym for Graphics Interchange Format, and again the clue is in the name: GIF was designed as a format for computer-created images – pictures that typically contain blocks of a single colour. GIF images can contain up to 256 different colours, which is usually fine for graphics you design yourself, but often gives poor results with photographs.

Deciding between JPEG and GIF
If you're unsure which is the best format for your image, create it with your graphics program set to use 16.7 million colours and save it in JPEG format. Next, reduce the number of colours to 256 and save again in GIF format. You can then compare the file sizes and picture qualities to decide which you want to use.

Figure 5.1

Paint Shop Pro, one of
the most popular
tools for creating Web
graphics.

In most graphics programs, saving an image in one of these formats is simple: choose **Save As** from the File menu, and select the format to use from the **Save As Type** list before you click the **Save** button. GIF images will be given the extension .gif, and JPEG images will have either .jpg or .jpeg.

Help! I'm artistically challenged!

We can't all be good artists, but modern graphics programs offer a lot of features to help the graphically inept produce amazing results. All it takes is the ability to recognise what's effective when you see it, and to spend some time getting to know your chosen software.

If you really can't be tempted into experimenting, though, there are plenty of ways to get your hands on free artwork for the Web. One of those is the Web itself, of course, and I've included a list of sites offering free graphics in Appendix B. If you have one of the WYSIWYG site-creation programs I mentioned in Chapter 1, you may be able to use the graphics provided with the software's templates. If you have an Office suite such as Microsoft Office, Microsoft Works or Lotus SmartSuite, you may be able to use images from their clipart galleries. You can also buy CD-ROMs containing thousands of examples of free use graphics, although the quality of these can vary enormously.

Finally, if you have a scanner you can scan photographs or graphics you've created on paper. Most good graphics programs have an **Acquire** option among their menus: clicking that will start the scanning process and load the finished result into the graphics software for touching up and saving in the correct format for the Web.

Adding images to a Web page

In Chapter 4 we looked at how to add a tiled background image to a Web page by adding the BACKGROUND attribute to the page's <BODY> tag. To do that, we used a relative URL giving the location of the image file relative to the location of the current Web page. Adding an **inline image** to the page works in just the same way, but there's a particular tag we use to do the job: the <IMG> tag.

+info

Inline image

This really just means 'an image on a Web page'. The word inline is often used to differentiate between an image displayed among the text of the page itself and an image used as a background or shown only if a link to the image is clicked.

Returning to our **index.htm** page, I've created an image to replace the heading at the top of the page and called it **banner.gif**. At the moment we're using the code below to put the heading on the page and set a font for it:

```
<FONT FACE="Verdana,Arial"><H1>The Computing Site
Directory</H1></FONT>
```

To replace that heading with the image, we can just replace that code with:

```
<IMG SRC="images/banner.gif"><P>
```

As usual, it's sensible to put the image file in the 'images' directory so that we'll know where to find it if we want to reuse it on future pages.

I've also added a `<P>` tag: the `<H1>` tag we were using before gave us a paragraph break after the heading which the `<IMG>` tag doesn't, so we need to add it ourselves. The result should look like Fig. 5.2.

The code above shows the `<IMG>` tag at its most basic. The SRC attribute (short for 'source') tells the browser where to find the image file you want to display, following the same rules as those for relative URLs covered in Chapter 3. The only thing the `<IMG>` tag does is to put an image on the page, so of all the possible attributes that could be added to this tag, the SRC attribute is the only one that *must* be included.

Aligning images

Like most of the HTML tags that add something new to the page (a paragraph, a heading, a horizontal rule, etc.), the `<IMG>` tag can have an ALIGN attribute to give you some control over where the image should be placed in relation to the items around it. In fact, you have a *lot* of control! The `<IMG>` tag's ALIGN attribute has more values available than any we've seen so far.

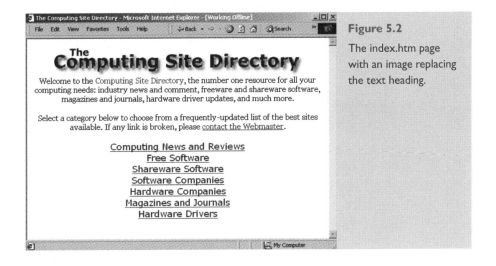

Figure 5.2

The index.htm page with an image replacing the text heading.

This attribute...	...does this
ALIGN=TOP	Aligns the top of the image with the top of the tallest item on the same line
ALIGN=TEXTTOP	Aligns the top of the image with the top of the tallest text on the same line. This is similar to ALIGN=TOP, but ignores anything on the line that isn't text
ALIGN=MIDDLE	Aligns the baseline of the text on the same line with the middle of the image
ALIGN=ABSMIDDLE	Aligns the middle of the line of text with the middle of the image
ALIGN=BOTTOM	Aligns the baseline of the text on the same line with the bottom of the image (ALIGN=BASE LINE does the same thing)
ALIGN=ABSBOTTOM	Aligns the bottom of the text with the bottom of the image. This is subtly different from ALIGN=BOTTOM: the *baseline* of the text is the line that characters like 'm', 'b' and 'r' sit on; characters like 'g' and 'y' drop below that line, and *bottom* is the lowest point that those characters reach
ALIGN=LEFT	Places the image on a new line against the left margin, with any text that follows the image wrapped to its right
ALIGN=RIGHT	Places the image against the left margin, with text wrapped to its left

Fig. 5.3 shows the result of using those ALIGN values in an image tag and placing a short line of text immediately after the image, such as <IMG SRC="images/box.gif" ALIGN=TOP>Align=TOP. I've put a <P> tag after the text in each case to create a reasonable gap between each image for clarity.

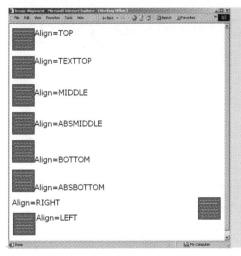

Figure 5.3

Fine-tuning the alignment of an image with a line of text.

Creating space around images

Using the ALIGN attribute, then, you can place the image roughly where you want it in relation to text or other images around it. What's needed is a bit more fine-tuning: after all, if you use ALIGN=ABSMIDDLE, the image will be butted right up against any text on the same line, and any text on the line preceding or following it.

The answer comes in the form of two more attributes which add some blank space around the image: HSPACE inserts space on either side of the image (*horizontally*), and VSPACE adds space above and below it (*vertically*). Just enter a number in pixels after the equals sign. As usual with attributes, if you only need to use one of these, there's no need to enter the other. In Fig. 5.4, the first image is inserted using <IMG SRC="images/box.gif" ALIGN=LEFT>; the second uses <IMG SRC="images/box.gif" ALIGN=LEFT VSPACE=10 HSPACE=15>.

Figure 5.4

Adding HSPACE and VSPACE attributes to the image tag in the second example adds blank space around the image.

Sizing images

Two of the most important <IMG> attributes are WIDTH and HEIGHT, with which you specify the dimensions of the image. If you've experimented with the image tag, you'll have noticed that your browser displays the image properly without these attributes, so you're probably wondering why you should go to the bother of finding and entering the image's dimensions.

At the moment you're looking at pages and images that are already on your computer – there's no downloading involved yet, so your browser loads the page and shows the images in the blink of an eye. When your page is on the Web and someone visits it, things work differently. When the browser arrives at an <IMG> tag with no WIDTH or HEIGHT attributes, it has to download the image, work out its dimensions and display it before it can decide how to lay out anything below the image. However, if the browser already knows how much space to reserve for the image, it can display an empty box until the image has downloaded, with the text correctly positioned around it.

Size matters!

If you need another good reason to add WIDTH and HEIGHT attributes, here it is: most browsers have an option to surf the Web without displaying images, and some people use it – pages load faster that way. Where images should appear on the page, the browser draws a 'placeholder' box containing a small icon. If you don't enter the dimensions of your images, those users will see a tiny box just large enough to contain the icon, which might upset your carefully-planned page layout. With the image dimensions entered, the placeholder box will be the size you wanted it to be.

You can find an image's dimensions easily by loading it into almost any good graphics program. In Paint Shop Pro, for example, you'll see them displayed in the bottom-right corner of the window. Make a mental note of the figures and add them to your tag like this:

```
<IMG SRC="images/banner.gif" WIDTH=503 HEIGHT=58>
```

Bear in mind that when you enter the dimensions of an image, the browser will take your word for it! In other words, the browser will resize the image to these dimensions regardless of what the original image was supposed to look like. This can be useful to increase or decrease the size of an image without creating a new version of it (or to create weird effects), but it's also a prime opportunity to make mistakes.

Using alternative text

Another useful attribute of the image tag is ALT, which specifies alternative text to display in place of the image. This is shown in the placeholder box on the page while the image is downloading, and in Internet Explorer and Netscape it's also displayed in a tooltip when the mouse moves over the image. For any visitors surfing without images displayed, this alternative text is the only clue to what that image would be if they could see it. So let's change the <IMG> tag in the index.htm page to add the correct dimensions and some alternative text. For visitors who've turned off image display, the page will look something like Fig. 5.5.

```
<IMG SRC="images/banner.gif" WIDTH=503 HEIGHT=58
ALT="The Computing Site Directory">
```

Images as links

In Chapter 3 you learnt how to create hypertext links to a Web page or file using the tag <A HREF="URL">clickable text</A>. But the clickable section that appears on the page doesn't have to be

Figure 5.5

With dimensions and alternative text added, the result is still meaningful when images are switched off.

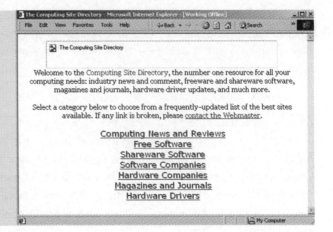

text: you can use an image instead. (In fact, you can use an image *and* text if you want to – just place it all between the opening and closing anchor tags as you want it to appear on the page.)

Let's replace the seven category-links on the index.htm page with button images to demonstrate this. I've created seven images, all with the same dimensions but with different text on each. In the section of the page containing the seven links, remove the <FONT> tags surrounding this block of code (we won't be displaying text there any longer, so they're redundant), and replace the text between each anchor tag with the appropriate image tag like this:

```
<P><A HREF="pages/news.htm"><IMG SRC="images/news.
jpg" WIDTH=185 HEIGHT=27></A><BR>
<A HREF="pages/free.htm"><IMG SRC="images/free.jpg"
WIDTH=185 HEIGHT=27></A><BR>
<A   HREF="pages/shareware.htm"><IMG   SRC="images/
shareware.jpg" WIDTH=185 HEIGHT=27></A><BR>
<A HREF="pages/softcomp.htm"><IMG SRC="images/soft-
comp.jpg" WIDTH=185 HEIGHT=27></A><BR>
<A HREF="pages/hardcomp.htm"><IMG SRC="images/hard-
comp.jpg" WIDTH=185 HEIGHT=27></A><BR>
```

```
<A HREF="pages/mags.htm"><IMG SRC="images/mags.jpg"
WIDTH=185 HEIGHT=27></A><BR>
<A HREF="pages/drivers.htm"><IMG SRC="images/driv-
ers.jpg" WIDTH=185 HEIGHT=27></A>
```

If you look at the page in your browser, you'll see that there's a problem: because we're using these images as links, the browser puts a border around each one in the same colour as hyperlinked text. The intention, of course, is to make it clear that these links, but on this page that should be obvious to anyone visiting; those borders just make the page look messy. Fortunately the <IMG> tag has another attribute, BORDER, that can help us out. We can add any number after the equals sign to set the thickness of the border, and zero is as valid as any other figure, so add a BORDER=0 attribute to each of the <IMG> tags. The result should look like Fig. 5.6.

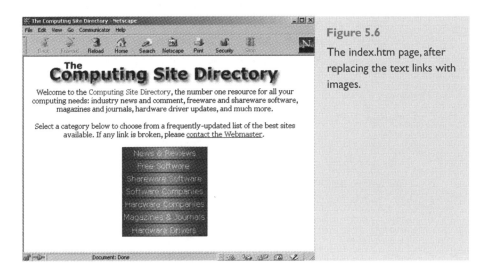

Figure 5.6
The index.htm page, after replacing the text links with images.

Border or no border?

The BORDER attribute can be added to any <IMG> tag, whether the image is a link or not. Non-linking images don't have a border by default, but you can create one by adding BORDER=1 to the tag (changing the number according to the thickness you want).

Looking around the Web, you'll notice that most site designers remove any borders from linking images. What matters most is that visitors can tell that an image is a link by looking at it, and the design of the image itself can usually get that across. Images containing text, for example, are generally expected to be links, as are any similarly-styled collections of images placed close together. If a page doesn't contain much in the way of hyperlinked text, most visitors will wave the mouse over images to see if they are links. In these situations, hypertext-coloured borders are unnecessary and could spoil the appearance of the page.

One of the few situations in which you might want to consider leaving the border intact is if you have a single image on the page some way from other images. For example, you may have an enve-lope icon at the bottom of the page acting as an email link (see Chapter 3). A border will help to draw attention to it as well as make it clear that it's a link.

6

Tables

- **Tables**
- **Meet the three tags that make a table**
- **Add style and colour to tables**
- **Use tables for simple data display or advanced page design**

If the word *tables* has got you thinking of rows and columns of dull-looking data, you're on the right lines: that's what HTML tables were originally planned for. But what makes them especially valuable to Web designers is that a cell in a table can contain anything at all – text, images, another table – and its contents can be aligned separately from anything else on the page. This gives a similar kind of design freedom to that found in desktop publishing. Even without getting to grips with style sheets (see Chapter 8) tables can be used to put things exactly where you want them on the page.

The obvious table

The easiest way to get started with tables is to create an 'obvious' table – a structured list of items grouped into rows and columns. This introduces the three tags that matter most in table creation: `<TABLE>`, `<TR>` and `<TD>`. Here's what each of those does:

`<TABLE>`	Used as a `<TABLE>...</TABLE>` pair to mark the beginning and end of a table.
`<TR>`	Used to mark the start and end of a row of cells in a table.
`<TD>`	Used to mark the start and end of a single cell in a row.

```
You can contact some imaginary people at the email
addresses below:
<TABLE BORDER=1>
<TR><TD>Anthony Turnip</TD><TD>anthony@turnipfam-
ily.com</TD></TR>
<TR><TD>Duane Pipe</TD><TD>dp@gutter.org</TD></TR>
<TR><TD>Bill Stickers</TD><TD>1045878@parkhurst.co.
uk</TD></TR>
</TABLE>
```

The code above creates the simple table shown in Fig. 6.1. The entire table is contained between `<TABLE>` and `</TABLE>` tags, and consists of three rows and two columns – in other words, each of the three rows contains two cells. I've placed the HTML code for each row on a separate line for clarity.

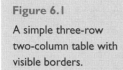

Figure 6.1

A simple three-row two-column table with visible borders.

You'll notice that I've added an attribute to the <TABLE> tag, BORDER="1". By default, an empty <TABLE> tag won't show a border around the table or any of its cells, and I wanted to make it obvious in the figure what effect those <TR> and <TD> tags were having. But it's the option of having those borders hidden that makes tables such a great page layout tool: to hide the table borders, either remove the BORDER="1" attribute or set its value to "0" instead.

Customising the <TABLE> tag

The BORDER attribute mentioned above is just one of the <TABLE> tag's attributes, and is simple to work with: set it to zero to hide the borders or to any positive number to create tables with thicker visible borders. It's worth noting that if you remove the BORDER attribute, although no borders will be shown, the table will be laid out as if the border were still there: setting it to 0 regains the space that would have been used for the border.

There are several other attributes you can add to the <TABLE> tag that affect the appearance of the whole table (see table overleaf).

Here are two modified examples of the table used in the earlier example. The first adds space around the table contents using cellpadding and cellspacing along with a thicker border; the second goes all out for compactness (Fig. 6.2):

This attribute...	...does this
ALIGN	Sets the alignment of the table on the page, using LEFT, CENTER or RIGHT. The default alignment is LEFT. (You can also do this by enclosing the table in <CENTER> or <DIV ALIGN=?> tags)
BGCOLOR	Sets the background colour for the entire table (although individual rows and cells can override this using their own BGCOLOR attributes, as we'll see later)
WIDTH	Sets the width of the table, either using an exact number of pixels or as a percentage of the browser's width, such as WIDTH="80%"
HEIGHT	Sets the height of the table. You wouldn't usually use this, since the browser will automatically create a table tall enough to display whatever data it contains
CELLPADDING	Sets the amount of space between a cell's four edges and its contents. The default is 1, so you can create extra space around a cell's contents using something like CELLPADDING="5"
CELLSPACING	Sets the amount of space between each cell in the table. The default spacing is two pixels

```
<TABLE   BORDER=5   CELLPADDING=5   CELLSPACING=10
ALIGN=CENTER BGCOLOR=ivory>
<TR><TD>Anthony Turnip</TD><TD>anthony@turnipfamily
.com</TD></TR>
<TR><TD>Duane Pipe</TD><TD>dp@gutter.org</TD></TR>
<TR><TD>Bill Stickers</TD><TD>1045878@parkhurst.co.
uk</TD></TR>
</TABLE>
<P>
<TABLE BORDER=0 CELLPADDING=0 CELLSPACING=0 BGCOLOR
=ivory>
```

```
<TR><TD>Anthony Turnip</TD><TD>anthony@turnipfamily.
com</TD></TR>
<TR><TD>Duane Pipe</TD><TD>dp@gutter.org</TD></TR>
<TR><TD>Bill Stickers</TD><TD>1045878@parkhurst.co.
uk</TD></TR>
</TABLE>
```

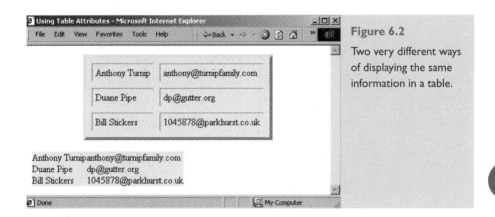

Figure 6.2

Two very different ways of displaying the same information in a table.

Table design using Internet Explorer

Internet Explorer versions 2 and upwards offer a few extra tricks with the <TABLE> tag. Most other browsers won't know what to do with these, so (as with all unsupported attributes) they'll ignore them.

BACKGROUND works like the same attribute in the <BODY> tag (see Chapter 4), letting you add a tiled image behind the content of all the table's cells.

BORDERCOLOR lets you set a colour to be used to draw the borders of the table and its cells. This will give a two-dimensional (flat) look to the table.

With BORDERCOLORLIGHT and BORDERCOLORDARK you can choose two separate colours to achieve your own style of three-dimensional table design: the first attribute sets the colour of the two lighter edges of the table or cell, the second sets the colour of the two darker edges.

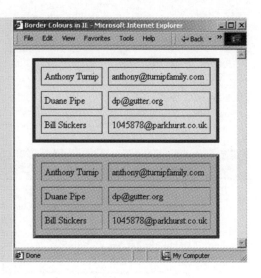

Rows: just containers for cells

Compared to the <TABLE> tag, the <TR> tag that starts a new row in a table can be dull, so we can skip through its possible attributes quickly. Because a row is just a container for cells, the attributes for a row can provide a quick way of creating settings that apply to every cell in that row. As we'll see later in this chapter, individual cells can still override these settings.

Along with the four attributes shown overleaf, you can also use Internet Explorer's BORDERCOLOR, BORDERCOLORLIGHT and BORDER-COLORDARK attributes mentioned on page 63, which will override the colours set in the <TABLE> tag.

This attribute...	...does this
ALIGN	Aligns the contents of cells in the row using LEFT, CENTER, RIGHT, or JUSTIFY, which are all self-explanatory, or CHAR, explained below
CHAR	If you use ALIGN=CHAR, the contents of each cell will be aligned to the first instance of a particular character in a cell's contents. Use CHAR="*character*" to specify the character used, such as CHAR="." to align numbers to a decimal point
VALIGN	Sets the vertical alignment of the content in all this row's cells, which can be TOP, MIDDLE, BOTTOM or BASELINE
BGCOLOR	Sets the background color of all the cells in this row. This overrides any BGCOLOR attribute used in the <TABLE> tag

Cells: what tables are all about

As you've seen in the examples earlier in this chapter, all the displayable content of a table appears in a cell – in other words, it comes between <TD> and </TD> tags The <TD> tag has a range of attributes to set the appearance of the cell and its content: WIDTH, HEIGHT, ALIGN, BGCOLOR, CHAR and VALIGN, all of which we've come across already, and the Internet Explorer-specific BACKGROUND, BORDERCOLOR, BORDERCOLORLIGHT and BORDERCOLORDARK. If any of these attributes is included in a <TD> tag, its value will take precedence over the same attribute used in the <TABLE> or <TR> tag. Along with those old favourites, the <TD> tag has two extra attributes of its own:

COLSPAN lets you join several cells together horizontally to create a single wide cell that spans several columns. For example, COLSPAN=3 creates a single cell of three columns.

ROWSPAN joins cells vertically to create a single cell spanning two or more rows, such as ROWSPAN=2.

Here's some code that shows how the COLSPAN and ROWSPAN attributes work, with the result shown in Fig. 6.4. The table contains four rows. The first row uses four <TD> tags to create four ordinary cells. In the second row there's a single <TD> tag with a COLSPAN=4 attribute making this cell span four columns (the width of this table). The third row also contains four cells, but the first <TD> tag includes a ROWSPAN=2 attribute: as long as there's another row below this one, this first cell will take the height of that row as well. Finally, the fourth row contains just three cells because the ROWSPAN attribute in the previous row has used one cell's worth of space.

```
<TABLE BORDER CELLPADDING=4 CELLSPACING=7 ALIGN=
CENTER>
<TR><TD>ROW1 CELL1</TD><TD>ROW1 CELL2</TD><TD>ROW1
CELL3</TD><TD>ROW1 CELL4</TD></TR>
<TR><TD COLSPAN=4>ROW2 CELL1</TD></TR>
<TR><TD ROWSPAN=2>ROW3 CELL1</TD><TD>ROW3 CELL2
</TD><TD>ROW3 CELL3</TD><TD>ROW3 CELL4</TD></TR>
<TR><TD>ROW4 CELL1</TD><TD>ROW4 CELL2</TD><TD>ROW4
CELL3</TD></TR>
</TABLE>
```

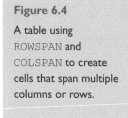

Figure 6.4

A table using ROWSPAN and COLSPAN to create cells that span multiple columns or rows.

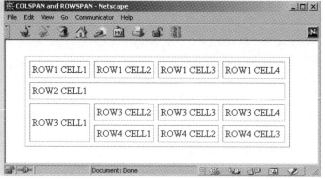

Tables in the real world

The examples we've used so far look a bit dull – they have the typical 'spreadsheet look' that the word *table* conjures up. Although tables obviously can be used to present tabular data in a Web page (and the first example below does just that, with some added style), their greatest value is in helping you to fine-tune your page layout.

A typical data table

The code below creates a table displaying a typical kind of tabular data, pictured in Fig. 6.5 (see p. 69). The data itself is dull, but there are a few points of interest about the table:

- In the first two rows I've used empty cells (`<TD></TD>`). There was nothing to be displayed in these cells and by leaving them blank no borders are shown around them. To show the borders, just include a non-breaking space (` `) between the opening and closing tags.

- The `<CAPTION>` tag makes an appearance. If used, this must immediately follow the `<TABLE>` tag (although there are several other ways to place a text caption above a table). The caption will be aligned to the top-centre by default, but you can choose between TOP, BOTTOM, LEFT and RIGHT for its ALIGN attribute.

- For effect in Internet Explorer, I've used the BORDERCOLORLIGHT and BORDERCOLORDARK attributes to swap the usual highlight and shadow colours, giving a raised-3D appearance. (I've cheated slightly by using a style sheet to set a few extra options. More about styles and style sheets in Chapter 8.)

```
<TABLE BORDER=1 BGCOLOR=lightgray BORDERCOLORLIGHT=
black  BORDERCOLORDARK=white  CELLSPACING=3  CELL-
PADDING=6 ALIGN=CENTER>
```

```
<CAPTION    ALIGN=LEFT><B>Company    Computers</B>
</CAPTION>
<TR>
      <TD></TD><TD COLSPAN=2 ALIGN=CENTER>PC</TD>
<TD COLSPAN=2 ALIGN=CENTER>Mac</TD>
</TR>

<TR>
      <TD></TD><TD>Desktop</TD><TD>Notebook</TD>
<TD>Desktop</TD><TD>Notebook</TD>
</TR>

<TR ALIGN=CENTER>
      <TD>Office    1</TD><TD>3</TD><TD>1</TD><TD>1
</TD> <TD>0</TD>
</TR>

<TR ALIGN=CENTER>
      <TD>Office    2</TD><TD>0</TD><TD>0</TD><TD>2
</TD> <TD>0</TD>
</TR>

<TR ALIGN=CENTER>
      <TD>Office    3</TD><TD>1</TD><TD>2</TD><TD>1
</TD> <TD>1</TD>
</TR>

<TR ALIGN=CENTER>
      <TD>Office    4</TD><TD>1</TD><TD>1</TD><TD>1
</TD> <TD>0</TD>
</TR>

</TABLE>
```

Page layout using tables

The next example uses a table for layout only. It consists of two rows, each with three cells. In the first row the middle cell is empty, and in the second row the two outer cells are empty (Fig. 6.6). The three cells that do contain something useful are all identical: their content is aligned to the centre and vertically aligned to the top.

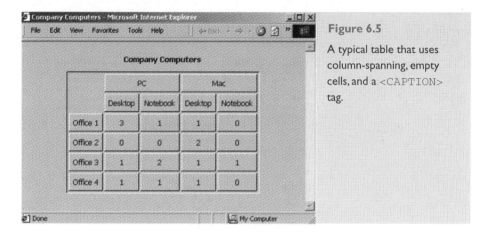

Figure 6.5

A typical table that uses column-spanning, empty cells, and a `<CAPTION>` tag.

```
<TABLE WIDTH="80%" ALIGN=CENTER BORDER="0">

<TR>
<TD VALIGN=TOP ALIGN=CENTER><IMG SRC="trials.gif"
WIDTH=169 HEIGHT=25><BR>Download anything you like
from this site, and try it FREE with no restric-
tions for up to 60 days! Then come back here and
buy it.</TD>
<TD></TD>
<TD VALIGN=TOP ALIGN=CENTER><IMG SRC="dev.gif"
WIDTH=169 HEIGHT=25><BR>The most popular area of
the site, devoted to widgets, tools and indispensa-
ble information for the software developer.</TD>
</TR>

<TR>
<TD></TD>
<TD VALIGN=TOP ALIGN=CENTER><IMG SRC="press.gif"
WIDTH=169 HEIGHT=25><BR>Press releases, company
information and contact details, product screen-
shots and packshots, distribution and reseller
partnerships, and related background information.
<TD></TD>
</TR>

</TABLE>
```

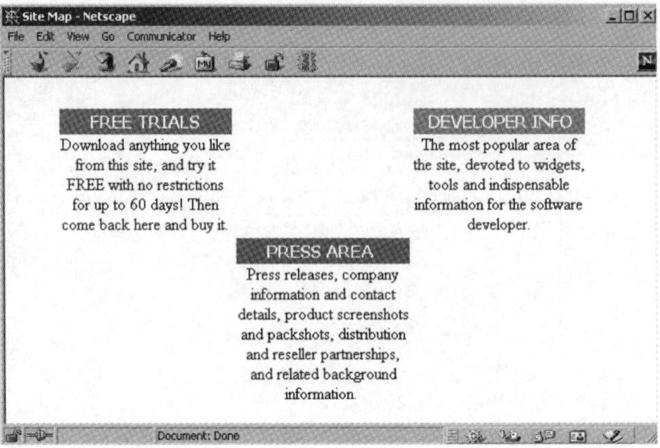

Figure 6.6

Without tables, it wouldn't be possible to create even simple-looking layouts like this.

The table itself is centred and limited to 80% of the window width. This means that each column could be about a quarter as wide as the browser, making the paragraphs of text wider and with fewer lines. If you wanted to keep each column to the same width as the image, just remove the `WIDTH=80%` attribute from the `<TABLE>` tag, and add a `WIDTH=169` attribute to the three `<TD>` tags containing text. The result will be a table of about 507 pixels wide containing three columns of fixed widths.

Setting *fixed* widths for tables or cells (widths in pixels rather than as percentages) is something to avoid, other than in cases where you know that the number of pixels you're specifying is small enough to fit into a reasonably-sized window. If you set particular widths for cells, remember that the width of a cell also sets the width for the whole column of cells it's contained in! If you try to give the top-left cell a width of 50 and the cell below it a width of 75, one or both will have to be ignored by the browser.

+info

Nested tables

A 'nested' table simply means one table created inside the cell of another. You'll come across 'nested framesets' in Chapter 7, which means a new set of frames created inside another frame.

Figure 6.7

Three rows, six columns, and a little judicious use of the BGCOLOR attribute.

A more advanced page layout

In the example below, the table has been used partly for effect as well as for layout: I've used the BGCOLOR attribute of the <TD> tag to create a stripe of colour, and the WIDTH and HEIGHT attributes to make sure the stripe is always 20 pixels wide (Fig. 6.7). I've also made use of the <TD> tag's WIDTH attribute in the first row: every cell but one has a fixed width, so when the browser's size is changed, the downward-pointing stripe at the right remains the same distance from the edge of the window (Fig. 6.8).

```
<TABLE    WIDTH="100%"    BORDER=0    CELLPADDING=0
CELLSPACING=0>
<TR>
<TD WIDTH=70> </TD>
<TD  WIDTH=20  BGCOLOR=RoyalBlue  HEIGHT=20> 
</TD>
<TD WIDTH=20> </TD>
<TD HEIGHT=75 VALIGN=MIDDLE><IMG SRC="cfisoftware
.jpg" WIDTH=366 HEIGHT=59></TD>
<TD WIDTH=20> </TD>
<TD WIDTH=120> </TD>
</TR>

<TR>
<TD WIDTH=70> </TD>
<TD BGCOLOR=RoyalBlue HEIGHT=20> </TD>
<TD COLSPAN=3 BGCOLOR= RoyalBlue HEIGHT=20 ALIGN=
CENTER>
```

```
<!-- ... LINKS INSERTED HERE... -->
</TD>
</TR>

<TR>
<TD COLSPAN=4 HEIGHT=7 ALIGN=RIGHT VALIGN=BOTTOM>
<FONT FACE="Tahoma,Arial,Sans-Serif" SIZE=2 COLOR=
RoyalBlue>
COOL FOCUS INTERNATIONAL LTD </FONT></TD>
<TD BGCOLOR= RoyalBlue HEIGHT=20> </TD>
                            <TD> </TD>
                            </TR>
                            </TABLE>
```

Planning complex table layouts
The golden rule is to work out the maximum number of cells you're going to need in a row before you start writing. In this example, the maximum was six cells (used in the first row). You can then make sure that every row contains that number of cells, remembering to include COLSPAN figures too. The third row, for instance, has one cell that spans four columns, plus two single cells.

Figure 6.8

The same page as in Fig. 6.7 with a visible table border to show how the rows and columns are arranged.

Create a Web site

7

Frames and windows

- **Make links open new browser windows**
- **Pick sensible names for your windows and frames**
- **Meet the all-important** `<FRAMESET>` **and** `<FRAME>` **tags**

rames give you a different way of structuring your site (or perhaps just a part of it) by splitting the browser window into two or
more 'panes', with each pane displaying a different document. In some
ways these frames function like separate windows – for example, a
frame can be scrolled if it contains a long document, or resized by
dragging its border, and opening a document in one frame doesn't
affect the documents displayed in any others.

Whether you use frames or not is a decision you'll have to make
about your site. Either way, you're not restricted to using a single
browser window – any time it makes sense to do so, you can force a
link to open in a new window. In this chapter we'll look at how
frames are created, what you can do to change their appearance and
behaviour and, most importantly, how you can make documents
open into particular frames or windows.

Working with multiple windows

Before we delve into the (slightly more complicated) world of frames, let's deal with windows. This gives us an easy way to get to grips with a new attribute of the `<A>` tag introduced in Chapter 3: the `TARGET` attribute. So far the only attribute we've used in the `<A>` tag is `HREF`, which gives the URL of the page to open. Because we haven't specified anything different, the new page replaces the old one in the browser when the link is clicked. The `TARGET` attribute lets you choose a different window (or, as you'll learn later, a particular frame) where the page should be opened, like this:

```
<A HREF="mypage.htm" TARGET=MyNewWindow>
```

When you click a link that includes the `TARGET` attribute in its anchor tag, the browser checks to see if a frame or window exists with the given name. If it does, the page is retrieved and opened into it; if it *doesn't* exist, the browser opens a new window and assigns the given name to it. The name isn't actually displayed anywhere in the window itself, so the name you choose can be as simple or as silly as you want it to be.

Let's take a simple example: make a new Web page containing the code below and call it 001.htm. Next, create three pages named 001a.htm, 001b.htm and 001c.htm, each containing some dummy text so that you can tell which page has opened where.

```
<HTML>
<HEAD>
      <TITLE>Main Window</TITLE>
</HEAD>

<BODY>
<H1>Main Window</H1>

<A HREF="001a.htm" TARGET=WindowOne>Open a window
called &quot;WindowOne&quot;</A><P>

<A HREF="001b.htm" TARGET=WindowTwo>Open a window
called &quot;WindowTwo&quot;</A><P>
```

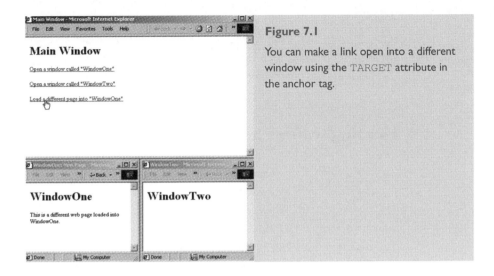

Figure 7.1

You can make a link open into a different window using the `TARGET` attribute in the anchor tag.

```
<A HREF="001c.htm" TARGET=WindowOne>Load a different
page into &quot;WindowOne&quot;</A><P>

</BODY>
</HTML>
```

Open 001.htm into your browser (it should look like the top window in Fig. 7.1) then follow these steps:

1   Click the first link. A new window will open containing the page you called 001a.htm. This is because the browser couldn't find an existing window called WindowOne, so it had to create one.

2   Click the second link. As in step 1, you should have another new window containing 001b.htm, for exactly the same reason.

3   Click the last link. Because you *do* now have a window called WindowOne, the browser doesn't need to open a new one. The page named 001c.htm opens into the window called WindowOne that was created in step 1.

While we're on the subject, opening new windows is a great way to annoy people! Most users know that they can shift-click a link to open it in a new window and prefer to choose for themselves. You might want to open links to other Web sites in a new window, especially if your site uses frames – it's not good manners to load someone else's site into one frame of your own site. Otherwise, good reasons for new windows are few and far between.

Naming frames and windows

Choosing names for frames and windows isn't complicated – the rules are minimal. Names mustn't start with an underscore (the underscore character is used by internal HTML names which we'll meet in a moment). Frame names are also case-sensitive, so **windowone** isn't the same thing as **WindowOne**. (This is well worth remembering: if you're working with frames and your pages persist in opening new windows rather than loading into your carefully-constructed set of frames, it's almost always a simple mistake like a missing capital letter in the name that's causing the problem!)

You can also refer to frames or windows using the five names supplied by HTML explained in the table below. Notice that these all start with an underscore and they're always lower-case.

This name...	...refers to
_self	The same frame or window as the one containing the link being clicked. If you don't use a TARGET attribute in the anchor tag, this is the frame or window used by default
_top	The window containing the link being clicked. If the window is split into frames, the frames will all be closed and the new document will replace them. (If the current window isn't split into frames, this means the same as _self)
_parent	The frame or window containing the parent document of the current frame; in other words, the document that created the frame being clicked. If the current frame doesn't have a parent, this defaults to _self. Rather

	than using _parent, it's simpler to refer to the required frame by whatever name you assigned it
_blank	A new window without a name. This will always result in a new window being opened: if you have three links with TARGET="blank", the result will be three extra windows open after all have been clicked
_new	A new window, but one that's reused by the browser. If you have three links with TARGET="_new", a new window will open when the first is clicked, and the second and third will open into that same window

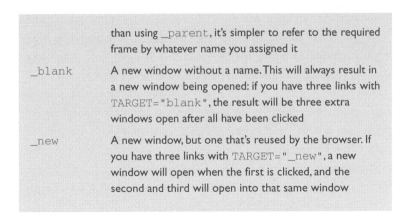

Figure 7.2

A typical framed site: two permanent navigation frames and a 'main' frame for the changing content.

Working with frames

A common use of frames is to split the window into two: the smaller frame contains the site navigation, and the larger frame displays the pages opened when the links are clicked (Fig. 7.2). Perhaps you can find a good reason to use a third frame – a fixed copyright notice, advertising banner display, company logo or secondary navigation – but you probably won't find any *good* reasons to use any more than that. Remember that for each frame you create there's a document to be downloaded when someone visits your site!

Frames don't suit every site, of course. If the content of more than one frame needs to change when links are clicked, the result might be more confusing for the user than sticking to a 'single-page view'. Instead of using frames, you could create a template file containing your logos, links, and anything else that should appear on every page, then create each page from that template, ensuring that the whole site will have a reassuringly consistent style and feel.

In Fig. 7.2 you can see a fairly typical use of frames, with the borders between the three frames clearly visible. The left and bottom frames contain links to other pages on the site, and the larger 'main' frame is where those pages will be displayed.

To build a site like this takes four Web pages. Three of those you can see in the three frames, and they're no different from any other Web page. The fourth page is the one that defines the **frameset** – it creates the frames and opens the required pages into them when the site is first shown. Appropriately enough, this is done using the `<FRAMESET>` tag.

Dividing the window: the `<FRAMESET>` tag

The framesetting page contains no displayable content at all. As a result, it has no `<BODY>...</BODY>` section either: the body of the page is replaced by the framesetting code, so a template for a framesetting page would look like this:

```
<HTML>
<HEAD>
      <TITLE>Untitled</TITLE>
</HEAD>
<FRAMESET>

</FRAMESET>
</HTML>
```

The `<FRAMESET>` tag tells the browser that the window is to be split into frames, but currently it isn't doing any more than that. To define how many frames we want and what size they should be, we have to add either of two attributes to the `<FRAMESET>` tag: `COLS` or `ROWS`. Which of these attributes you use depends on whether you want to split the window into columns or rows, but both are used in exactly the same way:

```
<FRAMESET COLS="width1, width2, width3">
```

or

```
<FRAMESET ROWS="height1, height2, height3">
```

In both code samples above, the window is split into three frames. In the first it's split into three columns of the specified widths; in the second it's split into three rows of the specified heights.

There are three different ways of specifying the width or height for a frame: as a fixed value in pixels, as a percentage of the entire width or height of the browser, or with an asterisk (*). The asterisk tells the browser to devote whatever space is left to this frame after creating the others. Each value is separated by a comma (and a space if you like to keep things tidy!). Here's an example `<FRAMESET>` tag that creates a window split like the one in Fig. 7.3. (Don't try typing this into your own page to test it just yet: you won't get the result I'm showing here, for reasons we'll come to in a moment.)

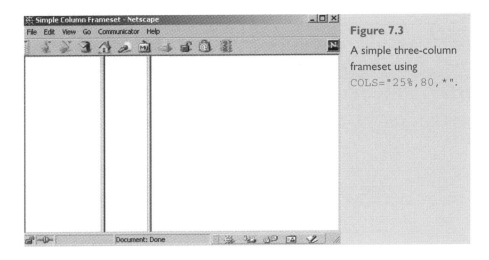

Figure 7.3
A simple three-column frameset using `COLS="25%,80,*"`.

```
<FRAMESET COLS="25%, 80, *">
```

That line of code has split the window into three columns. The left-most column occupies 25% of the size of the window; the middle column is fixed at 80 pixels wide; and the column on the right takes whatever space is left. If you resize the window, the width or the left-most frame will change slightly, the rightmost frame will change more, and the middle frame will remain at 80 pixels wide.

Let's take another example, this time using the ROWS attribute: the complete tag is `<FRAMESET ROWS="25%,*,25%">`, giving the result shown in Fig. 7.4. The first thing you'll notice is that the asterisk doesn't have to be the last value defined: the browser has quite happily split the window into three frames where the outer frames occupy 25% of the window's size and the centre frame takes the rest. That leads to another point: why not just put 50% where the asterisk is? In the example above we could certainly do that and the result would be the same. However, it's good practice to get into the habit of always including an asterisk: that way there's never any risk of creating a frameset adding up to more or less than 100%.

Avoid fixed frame sizes!

There's only one instance when you might consider specifying a frame's width or height in pixels: when you know the maximum size of the content it will display (for example, an image of a particular size) and if the size is a lot smaller than the user's browser window would ever reasonably be. Otherwise stick to percentage values and always use at least one asterisk in each <FRAMESET> tag.

+info

Using more than one asterisk

Using multiple asterisks is valid. After the percentage values and pixel values have been determined, the remaining space is split equally between the asterisk values. For instance, the code `<FRAME-SET ROWS="25%,*,25%,*">` would split the browser into four identical rows. The code `<FRAMESET ROWS="*,*,*,*">` would do exactly the same: as there are no numbers to work with, the browser splits its remaining 100% into four equal portions.

Filling and naming: the `<FRAME>` *tag*

I've been cheating a bit in the examples from the previous section. Although the `<FRAMESET>` tag and its ROWS or COLS attribute is required, alone it won't produce the examples in the figures. A frame can't be empty – it has to con-

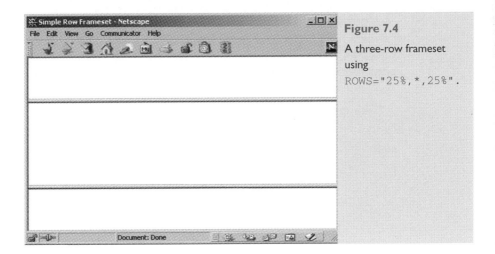

Figure 7.4

A three-row frameset using
`ROWS="25%,*,25%"`.

tain a document – and there's nothing in the code we've seen so far to load any documents. For this step we need to add a `<FRAME>` tag for each frame we created in the `<FRAMESET>` tag, like this:

```
<HTML>
<HEAD>
      <TITLE>My Frameset</TITLE>
</HEAD>
<FRAMESET COLS="25%, *">
      <FRAME SRC="leftframepage.htm">
      <FRAME SRC="mainframepage.htm">
</FRAMESET>
</HTML>
```

Two frames are defined in the `<FRAMESET>` tag, so two `<FRAME>` tags are needed to load documents into each. The first `<FRAME>` tag corresponds to the first value in the COLS or ROWS attribute (`"25%"` in this example), the second `<FRAME>` tag to the second value, and so on. The SRC attribute of the `<FRAME>` tag is short for 'source': it works in the same way as the SRC attribute of the `<IMG>` tag, covered in Chapter 5, specifying the URL of the page to be loaded into the frame.

The page in the example code above is complete: you can load this page into a browser and the two frames will be shown. Provided the pages specified in the <FRAME> tags really do exist, they'll be loaded into the frames, otherwise the frames will contain 'page not found' messages.

We're off to a good start, but we're missing out on something important: the frames don't have names, so if one of the pages contains links, we can't target the links to the other frame. That's easily fixed using another attribute of the <FRAME> tag, **NAME**, like this:

```
<HTML>
<HEAD>
        <TITLE>My Frameset</TITLE>
</HEAD>

<FRAMESET COLS="25%, *">
        <FRAME SRC="leftframepage.htm" NAME="left">
        <FRAME SRC="mainframepage.htm" NAME="main">
</FRAMESET>
</HTML>
```

+info

Title fight

With several Web pages open, each of which has its own title, you might expect things to get a bit hit-or-miss in the <TITLE> tag department. In fact, when pages are displayed in a framed environment, their <TITLE> tag is ignored completely and the title of the framesetting page is used exclusively. This makes your choice of title for that page all the more important since it remains permanently on show.

Now we can add some links to the page named leftframepage.htm, making sure we include the attribute TARGET="main" in the <A> tags. When one of those links is clicked, the page it refers to will open in the larger frame we called *main* (Fig. 7.5).

Customising your frames

The SRC attribute of the <FRAME> tag is *required* and must specify the URL of the document to load into the frame when it's created. The NAME attribute is optional, but you'll

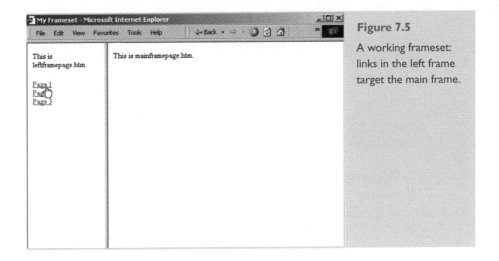

Figure 7.5

A working frameset:
links in the left frame
target the main frame.

need to include it for any frame that you need to target from a link.
Apart from those, there are a few extra attributes that you can add
to the <FRAME> tag to customise its behaviour or appearance.

This attribute...	...does this
MARGINWIDTH	Takes a value in pixels to set the width of the left and right margins of a frame
MARGINHEIGHT	Takes a value in pixels to set the height of the top and bottom margins of a frame
SCROLLING	Takes a setting of auto, yes or no as to whether the user should be able to scroll the frame. The default setting is auto, meaning that scrollbars will be added to the frame if the content is too wide or long to fit the frame; yes means that scrollbars will always be visible; no means that the frame can never be scrolled. Avoid using no unless you're absolutely sure that the content of a frame will always be fully visible without the need to scroll though it

NORESIZE	By default all frames can be resized by dragging them. To prevent a frame from being resized by the user, include this empty attribute in its <FRAME> tag
FRAMESPACING	In Internet Explorer only, this attribute can be used to create blank space around a frame by entering a value in pixels

A complex frameset example

So far all our frameset examples have been simple ones: we've split the browser into columns or rows, but we haven't tried to combine the two. A good candidate for a more complex frameset is our long-running 'Computing Site Directory' site, last seen at the end of Chapter 5. Fig. 7.6 shows the result we want to achieve; for complex framesets, as with complex tables, it's a good idea to scribble a rough diagram of what you're trying to create before you start.

Figure 7.6

A rough mock-up of the frameset we want to create.

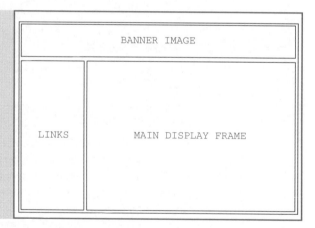

Now we hit the first complication: do we use the ROWS or COLS attribute in the <FRAMESET> tag? The window is clearly split into two rows, the lower row containing the two larger frames, but there's also a column split between the two large frames. The answer is to see whether any frames stretch from the extreme left to the extreme right of the window: if they do, use ROWS; if they don't, use COLS. In this case, the top frame fills the entire width of the browser, so we'll use ROWS.

The top frame is only going to contain the banner image: it's a fixed size (58 pixels high), so we can set a pixel value for the height of that frame, allowing a few extra pixels for frame and page margins (and testing carefully in all browsers to make sure the frame really is tall enough for the image!). The remainder of the window is left for the frames below. So far, then, we can enter the following code into the page:

```
<FRAMESET ROWS="80,*">
        <FRAME NAME="top"SRC="banner.htm"SCROLLING=NO
NORESIZE>
        <!-- more code here -->
</FRAMESET>
```

Now we've got a line missing from the code. Normally we'd put a second <FRAME> tag there to create the frame that forms the second row, but in our mock-up we've got two frames in that row. That means we need another <FRAMESET> tag instead. Putting one frameset inside another in this way is known as a **nested frameset**. We don't have to do anything any differently though: we just treat the remaining space as if it were the entire browser window. We want to split the space into two columns, so we'll use the COLS attribute in this frameset tag:

```
<FRAMESET ROWS="80,*">
        <FRAME NAME="top"SRC="banner.htm"SCROLLING=NO
NORESIZE>
        <FRAMESET COLS="220,*">
                <FRAME NAME="left"SRC="links.htm">
                <FRAME NAME="main"SRC="home.htm">
        </FRAMESET>
</FRAMESET>
```

The left frame will contain our linking images which, like the banner, are a fixed size. That means we can set a fixed width of 220 pixels for the left frame, with the remainder of the window devoted to the main display frame. The resulting code goes in our **index.htm** page, straight after the closing `</HEAD>` tag.

Having created the frameset in index.htm, we need to create the three pages to be loaded into the frames. Here are the steps to take:

1 Make a page called **banner.htm** which contains just the `<IMG>` tag for the banner image between `<CENTER>` tags. You can also copy the `<BODY>` tag from the original index page to this one.

2 Make a page called **links.htm**. Into that, copy the block of code that put the linking button-images on the page, once again between `<CENTER>` tags and using the same `<BODY>` tag. Add `TARGET="main"` to each anchor tag so that all the links open into the frame called *main*.

3 Make a page called **home.htm** that uses the same `<BODY>` and `<FONT>` tags as the original index, and move the two introductory paragraphs into it (Fig. 7.7).

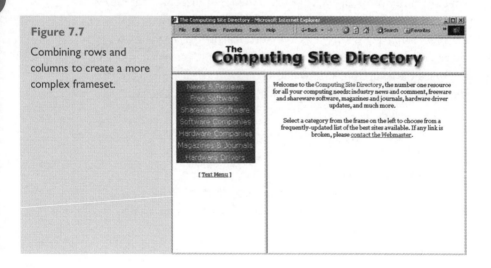

Figure 7.7

Combining rows and columns to create a more complex frameset.

8

Style sheets

- **What are style sheets, and are they worth bothering with?**

- **How to create simple but useful style sheets**

- **CSS property names and measurements**

- **How to customise and create your own style classes**

- **How to move styles into separate files for complete flexibility**

By now you've probably realised that HTML isn't much like desktop publishing in Serif PagePlus or presentation graphics in Microsoft PowerPoint: you can't determine precisely where items will be placed on the page, and if you can get everything the way you want it in one browser, there's little chance of it looking exactly the same in another.

That's not a limitation of HTML, though: the whole point of a markup language like HTML is that content is king and stylistic options are only needed to make the meaning of the content clearer. A heading doesn't need to be 30-point extra-bold Arial in green and indented by 26 pixels to be recognised as a heading, it just needs to be bigger.

The trouble is, you want your heading to be 30-point extra-bold Arial in green, and you don't care how a markup language is meant to be used! If that means wrapping every heading on your site in <FONT>

tags, you'll do it. And if redesigning your site means editing 500 identical font tags, you'll do that too. But wouldn't it be nice if there were a quicker, easier and more reliable way to exert some control over appearance? Looks like you've come to the right chapter…

What are style sheets?

The 'quicker, easier and more reliable way' comes in the form of **Cascading Style Sheets** or CSS (often just referred to as *style sheets*). Style sheets let you specify just once that a heading should be 30-point Arial in green, and apply that style to a whole page or, better still, an entire site. The result is a faster and more economical way to give a consistent appearance to a set of Web pages, and gives you as little as one line of code to edit if you decide that all the headings on your site would actually look better in blue. Not only that, style sheets give much more control over the positioning and styling of any element on the page than HTML alone can offer, as you can see from Fig. 8.1.

A 'style sheet' itself is pretty much what it sounds like: a list of named styles known as **rules** that you define yourself and can then apply by name to elements on the page. Styles can be created in three different ways:

Figure 8.1

Style sheets at work: try doing this with ordinary HTML!

1 An **external style sheet** is a separate document containing the defined style rules. This document can be used by any Web page that should share those styles, by **linking** the style sheet to the document.

2 An **embedded style sheet** is a list of style rules included in the head section of the Web page itself. Those styles are accessible to that page only.

3 **Inline styles** are styles added as attributes to ordinary HTML tags using a `<P STYLE="`*style info*`">` or `<H1 STYLE="`*style info*`">` `tag`.

Creating a simple style sheet

To start with we'll stick with *embedded* styles, style sheets included in a Web page rather than in a separate document. To define style rules in a Web page we use the `<STYLE>...</STYLE>` tag pair somewhere in the head of the page like this:

The age-old compatibility question
By now you'll probably be expecting this: style sheets don't have universal support among browsers. The most reliable support comes from versions 4 and higher of Internet Explorer and Netscape, and Opera 3 or higher. Internet Explorer 3 had some support, but not enough to be relied on. Even now, some style properties are supported by one browser and not by another. The answer, as always, is to test your pages in the browsers that matter before publishing them, and (if you choose to) include the minimum amount of stylistic HTML to make your pages look okay in older browsers such as Netscape 3.

```
<HTML>
<HEAD>
   <TITLE>Untitled</TITLE>
   <STYLE TYPE="text/css">
   <!--
   style rules here
   -->
   </STYLE>
</HEAD>
```

One of the first things you'll notice about the added code is that everything between the opening and closing `<STYLE>` tags is commented out by being enclosed between `<!--` and `-->` tags (see the section on Commenting HTML code in Chapter 3). This prevents errors in older browsers that don't recognise the `<STYLE>` tags. You might expect new browsers to ignore the style we put between those comments too, but they don't. Code within the `<STYLE>` tags is written in the 'language' of CSS, which is different from HTML. Browsers that understand CSS switch into that mode when they see the `<STYLE>` tag, and the `<!--` tag is meaningless in CSS so the browser ignores it and skips straight to what follows.

Now let's define a style rule for headings. If you wanted every heading in your page to use the Verdana font, the HTML way of doing that would be:

```
<FONT NAME="Verdana,Arial,sans-serif"><H1>My First
Heading</H1></FONT>
etc...
<FONT NAME="Verdana,Arial,sans-serif"><H1>My Second
Heading</H1></FONT>
etc...
```

Let's create a style rule for that instead:

```
<HTML>
<HEAD>
   <TITLE>Untitled</TITLE>
   <STYLE TYPE="text/css">
   <!--
   H1 {font-family: Verdana,Arial,sans-serif}
   -->
   </STYLE>
</HEAD>
<BODY>
<H1>My First Heading</H1>
etc...
```

```
<H1>My Second Heading</H1>
etc...
</BODY>
</HTML>
```

The added line (shown in bold type) creates a style rule for the `<H1>` tag. The rule specifies that the `<H1>` tag should use the Verdana font if possible, so all `<H1>` tags on the page will do so without the need for font tags or repetition.

The format of a style rule always follows the same simple format:

tag-name { property1: value1; property2: value2; property 3: value3 }

The tag-name (minus its < and > signs) starts the rule, and is followed by property-names and their values, all enclosed in curly brackets. There's a colon between the property-name and its value, and there's a semi-colon between each name-and-value pair (the semi-colon is optional after the last value). The use of spaces and carriage returns is ignored, as in HTML, and the property names aren't case-sensitive.

If you copy the code above into a new page and open it in your browser, you'll see that everything else about the headings remains unchanged: they have the same colour, alignment and size as they would if we'd specified the font using a `<FONT>` tag. When you specify a value for a particular property, you're effectively overriding its default value; any properties you leave out will remain at their defaults.

Let's test that by adding another property to our H1 rule. At the moment the headings in your browser are probably black, so change the style rule to this (not forgetting the semi-colon after the `font-family` property):

```
H1 {font-family: Verdana,Arial,sans-serif; color:
navy}
```

Look at the result in your browser now, and you'll find that the headings are navy blue.

A few CSS property names

Creating a style rule for a tag isn't difficult: all you're lacking at this stage is the property names to use. Here's a list of some of the most useful ones:

This property...	...does this
font-family	Specifies the names of the fonts to be used, in order of preference, such as font-family: Arial, Helvetica, sans-serif
font-style	Sets the style of the font, with a choice of normal or italic
font-weight	Sets the weight of the font, with a choice of normal or bold, or a fixed weight of 100, 200, 300, 400, 500, 600, 700, 800 or 900. (Normal is 400, Bold is 700. Others may actually be ignored in some browsers.)
font-size	Sets the size of font. There are named sizes (large, medium, small, x-large, x-small, xx-large and xx-small) or sizes can be given using one of the CSS units of measurement covered below
text-decoration	A choice of none, underline, overline or line-through
text-align	Aligns text with a choice of left, center, right, or justify
letter-spacing	Sets the amount of space between each letter
color	Sets the foreground colour of text contained in the element. A hex colour (color: #00FF00), a colour name (color: lime) or an RGB colour (color: RGB(0,255,0))
background-color	Sets the background colour of an element using the same syntax as the color property. (You can also use the shorter property-name, background.)

left	Sets the position of the left edge of the element
top	Sets the position of the top edge of the element
border-style	Sets the style of border shown, with a choice of solid, double, groove, ridge, inset, outset, dotted and dashed
border-width	Sets the width of borders, with a choice of thin, medium, thick, a percentage value, or a CSS unit of measurement

That's not an exhaustive list of properties by any means, but it should give you plenty to go on with. Not every property can be used with every HTML tag (or *element*), of course: the font-style and text-align properties clearly have no place in an image tag, for instance, because an image doesn't have associated text, but they could be used in a style rule for a paragraph or a table.

+info

Using unsupported property names

As with HTML tag attributes, if a browser doesn't recognise a property name you enter, it will just ignore it. That may be because you've experimented with an inappropriate property in an element (such as text-decoration for IMG elements), or because you've made a spelling mistake.

CSS measurement units

Quite a number of properties cover widths, positions, indents and sizes – properties that need a numerical value – and style sheets let you specify these as precisely as you want to by giving you a choice of units of measurement that you can use interchangeably. The two you'll probably want to use most are pixels (notated as px) and points (pt), but any unit in the table overleaf can be used in any numerical property.

Unit name	Unit notation	Meaning
Pixels	px	A pixel is a single dot on the screen
Points	pt	A point is $\frac{1}{72}$ inch, the unit used to measure the height of fonts
Picas	pc	12 points
Ems	em	The width of the current font's letter *m*
Exes	ex	The height of the current font's letter *x*
Millimetres	mm	A figure in millimetres
Centimetres	cm	A figure in centimetres (10 mm)
Inches	in	A figure in inches (2.54 cm)

Building a complete style sheet

A complete style sheet is simply a list of the rules you want to apply to particular HTML elements. As is usual for anything appearing in the head of a page, the order you define them doesn't matter. The code below shows an example of a style sheet containing five style rules. Let's look at each rule individually to see what it does, then see the result in a Web page:

```
<STYLE TYPE="text/css">
<!--
BODY{font-family:Georgia,serif;font-size:11pt;
background-color:ivory;color:navy;margin:2pc}
A{font-weight:900;text-decoration:none}
I{background-color:navy;color:ivory}
TD{font-family:Georgia,serif;font-size:11pt;text-
align:center}
H1,H2{font-family:Tahoma,sans-serif;color:maroon}
-->
</STYLE>
```

- The BODY rule is setting a default font and size for the whole page (the equivalent of enclosing the body of the page between <FONT>...</FONT> tags in HTML). It also sets the page's background colour to pale yellow (equivalent to <BODY BGCOLOR="ivory">) and the text colour to navy blue (equivalent to <BODY TEXT="navy">). Finally we've used margin:2pc: we can use this instead of using the separate margin-left/right/top/bottom properties to set the same 2-pica margin around all four edges at once.

- The A rule specifies that any links should have a font-weight of 900 (the 'heaviest' available weight of bold text). It also sets text-decoration to 'none', which, for ordinary text, would be redundant. For links, which are automatically underlined, it removes the underlining.

- The I rule specifies that any italic text in the page (text enclosed between <I>...</I> tags) should have a navy background and pale yellow text – the opposite of other text on the page.

- The TD (table data) rule doesn't appear to do anything very useful: apart from setting the text alignment it just repeats the same font-family and size properties we've already set in the BODY rule. However, you may remember from Chapter 6 that table cells in Netscape and Opera don't inherit the font set for the rest of the page, so you had to include an identical <FONT> tag in every cell. Netscape 4 has the same problem even when the font is set in a CSS BODY style, but this time we can get around it far more economically: we just add a rule specifying the font to use in any TD tag.

- Finally there's a rule marked for H1, H2. This is a valid way of creating a rule that will be applied to two different tags. In this case, any H1 or H2 heading we use in the page will be shown using the specified font type and colour.

To see the result of using this style sheet, open your template file to make a new Web page, and copy the code above into its head section. Then copy this code into its body section and look at the result in your browser (Fig. 8.2).

95

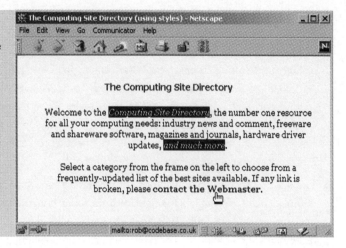

Figure 8.2

Combining a complete style sheet with a complete Web page.

```
<BODY>
<H1>The Computing Site Directory</H1>
<TABLE BORDER=0><TR><TD>
Welcome to the <I>Computing Site Directory</I>, the
number one resource for all your computing needs:
industry news and comment, freeware and shareware
software, magazines and journals, hardware driver
updates, <I>and much more</I>.

<P>Select a category from the frame on the left
to choose from a frequently-updated list of the
best sites available. If any link is broken, please
<A HREF="mailto:rob@codebase.co.uk">contact the
Webmaster</A>.
</TD></TR></TABLE>
</BODY>
```

Creating your own style classes

The examples we've used so far allow flexibility, but we're still a bit restricted. We can set a style rule for <P> tags that determines what a paragraph of text should look like, but what if we want an occasional paragraph of text to look different?

The solution is actually very easy: we can *extend* the existing tags by creating our own named variations on them. Imagine we have already defined a fairly plain-looking paragraph style like this:

```
P {font-family:Arial;font-size:11pt;color:navy}
```

We'd also like our document to contain a couple of paragraphs that have a border around them. We can do it like this:

```
P.boxed {border:1px solid;padding:5px}
```

We've created a new **style class** based on `P` and named 'boxed'. All we had to do was put a dot after the basic tag name, followed by the name we wanted to use for the new style.

To use the class we've defined, we add a `CLASS` attribute to the basic tag in the form `CLASS="classname"`. The `CLASS` attribute is a generic attribute that can be added to any tag that places something on the page or marks out a page section – `<A>`, `<IMG>`, `<P>`, `<TD>`, and so on.

In Fig. 8.3, the text is split into three paragraphs, each enclosed between `<P>` and `</P>` tags. The second paragraph differs from the other two in just one respect: its opening `<P>` tag is `<P CLASS="boxed">`. As a result, this paragraph inherits all the

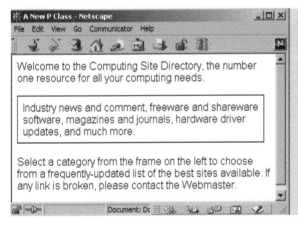

Figure 8.3

You can define any number of classes based on existing tags and refer to them by name in the `CLASS` attribute when you want to use them.

properties of an ordinary HTML paragraph, and the font family, size and colour set in the first rule for the P tag. It also has the border and padding we've defined for any paragraph using the 'boxed' class.

In a similar way we could define a class of bold text that's always green by creating a new bold-text class called 'green' (or something much less appropriate if you prefer – the choice of name is up to you!).

```
B.green {color: lime}
...
Here is some <B CLASS="green">green bold text</B>.
```

Using and reusing external style sheets

So far we've only worked with one way of getting style information into a Web page, the **embedded** style sheet. The problem with putting style information in the head of a Web page like this is that the style rules you create are only accessible to that page – if the rest of your pages should look the same, you'll need the same set of style rules in those pages too. And, needless to say, if you want to restyle your entire site, you've got to edit the style rules in every page.

A far more efficient way of working is to create **external** style sheets which can be used by any Web page on your site. And it's easier than falling off a log: just move all the rules into a separate text file, leaving out the <STYLE> and </STYLE> tags and the comment tags, and give the resulting file a **.css** extension. You now have an external style sheet!

The second step is to *link* that style sheet to a Web page. That just takes a single line of code in the head of the page:

```
<HTML>
<HEAD>
   <TITLE>Untitled</TITLE>
   <LINK REL=STYLESHEET TYPE="text/css" HREF="mystyle
.css">
</HEAD>
```

The <LINK> tag tells the browser that an external file is to be read in conjunction with this page; the REL attribute specifies the *relationship* of the Web page to the external file; and the TYPE attribute specifies its MIME type as "text/css" (just as in the <STYLE> tag). The only part of the tag you need to change is the HREF attribute which gives the absolute or relative URL of the style sheet to be read.

Apart from the fact that the style rules only need to be downloaded once when a visitor arrives at your site, using an external file will greatly improve your life as a Web designer. You can link this style sheet to every Web page on your site, refer to style classes named in the file, and you can restyle the entire site just by making a few simple changes to this one file.

Using inline styles

Once in a while you'll want to do something special in just one Web page, something that needs CSS to accomplish, such as making text overlap an image. You could create a named class (something like **.overlap**) in your external style sheet, or add it as an embedded style in the head of the page, but if you really do need it only once it would be simplest just to type it into the tag it applies to.

This is known as an **inline style**: it applies CSS properties and values to the current tag using a STYLE attribute. As with the CLASS attribute, mentioned earlier, the STYLE attribute can be used with any tag that places content on the page or marks out a section. So to move some text upwards so that it overlaps an image placed above, you might place it between <DIV> tags containing an inline style, like this:

```
<IMG SRC="fan.jpg"WIDTH=248 HEIGHT=338>
<DIV  STYLE="margin-left:165px;margin-top:-210px;
font-size:24pt"><B><I>Everybody needs fans!</I></B>
</DIV>
```

The STYLE attribute is followed by an equals sign and the list of **property: value** pairs you want to apply, separated by semi-colons in the usual way with the whole lot enclosed in quotes (Fig. 8.4). Better still, this effect will look the same in each of the major browsers!

Fun with <DIV> and <SPAN>

Two tags that are purpose-built to use inline styles are the <DIV> and <SPAN> tags. The <SPAN> tag is used to apply a style to some ordinary text within a paragraph, like this:

```
Here's some normal text. <SPAN
STYLE=  "background:  blue">
Here  some  text  with  a  blue
background.</SPAN>  And  more
normal text.
```

Using the <SPAN> tag here simply applies a blue background to the text it encloses. It doesn't alter the layout of the paragraph at all. (You can use <SPAN CLASS="..."> to apply a named style class instead if you need to.) There's really only one situation in which <SPAN> is useful:

Figure 8.4

Using an inline style to force text to overlap an image.

when you want to apply an effect that isn't available in HTML, as in the example above.

The `<DIV>` tag is a lot more useful. If you wanted to apply an inline style that indented a large chunk of content by 50 pixels, and that 'chunk' included images, paragraphs and headings, you'd have to apply the same inline `STYLE` attribute to all of them, or define a style class and apply it to each tag using `CLASS` attributes. In other words, you're repeating yourself, and in any form of programming you should avoid doing that if possible: it makes the code larger and increases the risk of mistakes.

`<DIV>` works a lot like the `<BODY>` tag, in that any amount of content and other tags can be placed between its opening and closing tags so you can use this tag, with a `STYLE` attribute to define an inline style, to enclose that chunk of content. The `<DIV>` tag automatically starts a new line for the chunk of content and whatever follows the closing `</DIV>` tag – in other words, it makes a *division* between this block and its surroundings. (It also supports an optional `ALIGN` attribute, as I mentioned at the end of Chapter 2.) So a simple solution to our 'chunk indentation' problem would be something like this:

```
<DIV STYLE="margin-left: 50px; color: blue">
<IMG SRC="blah.gif">
<P>Blah blah blah...
<H1 STYLE="color: red">Big Blah</H1>
<P>More blah
</DIV>
```

There are two extra points of interest to the code above. First, although I've included a `color` property in the style, the `<IMG>` tag clearly doesn't support it. No problem – it's gracefully ignored for that tag and applied only to the textual content. Second, I've added a `color` property to the heading tag. This has greater priority than the same property in the division tag, so the heading will be red.

9

From hard disk to Web

- How to find and choose a Web hosting company
- Register your own domain name
- Get your site online using FTP
- Testing times – checking and troubleshooting your new site
- Promotion and feedback: search engines, banners and guestbooks

 Now that you know something about HTML, it's time to put on your hard hat and start building. But what happens when you've finished? How does your site get on to the Web? What will its URL be? And how will anyone else know it's there? In this chapter, we'll find the answers to all those questions and more.

The perfect host

Once your site is finished, you're ready to publish it on the Web. Publishing your site means copying all the files in the 'Site' directory on your hard disk to a similar directory on a Web server. That directory will have its own URL, formed from the name of the server and the directory's name, and that's the URL you'll give out to anyone who'll listen when you promote the site. It may not be a very good URL (too long, hard to remember, difficult to type, and so on) so you might want to pick your own *domain name* – we'll look into that later in the chapter.

First, you need someone to **host** your site – in other words, you need to find a company willing to provide space on their Web servers for it. As you already have an Internet connection, your service provider probably includes free Web space, so you've got that question answered already. If your ISP doesn't give you space for free, don't pay yet – believe it or not, there are companies out there that provide Web space completely free. Here are a few to try:

● **GeoCities** at http://uk.geocities.yahoo.com

● **EasySpace** at http://www.easyspace.com

● **Tripod** at http://www.tripod.com

● **FortuneCity** at http://www.fortunecity.com (Fig. 9.1)

There are some negative aspects to these free hosting companies. First, if the company deletes all your files, or their computers go down for six months and your site becomes unavailable, you're not in

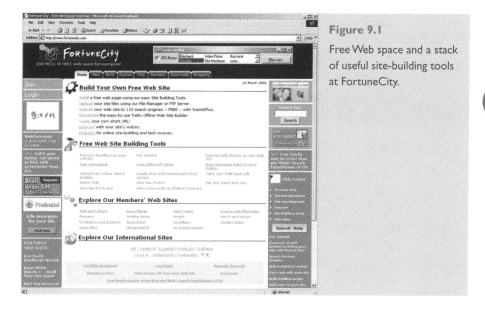

Figure 9.1

Free Web space and a stack of useful site-building tools at FortuneCity.

a strong position to complain. Second, you may find that your pages and graphics are unusually slow to load. Third, you might be required to display the hosting company's choice of banner ads or logo on your pages (or the company may insert these auto-matically at the server); in some cases, a pop-up advertising window will open whenever a link is clicked. Be sure to look at few sites belonging to other users of the service before committing yourself!

The name game

Whether you buy Web space, use Web space provided by your ISP, or go to one of the free-space providers, you'll be given a username for the account and a directory with the same name on their server (perhaps prefixed with a ~ symbol) such as www.mywebhost.com/ ~myname, and that will be the URL of your Web site. It's long, it isn't easy to remember (particularly if it contains numbers as well as let-ters), and it gives a poor first impression of your site. Fortunately, you have a couple of options available to replace this with something shorter and snappier.

The first and most popular option is to register your own domain name, such as myname.co.uk. There are dozens of companies in the UK selling domain names on the Web, and you can simply choose the name you want, pay for it, and then decide how you want to use it. The price you pay gives you ownership of the domain name for two years, with an option to renew it annually when the two year period is up. There are some variations in pricing depending upon the **top-level domain** you choose (a .co.uk domain can be bought for under £10 if you shop around, whereas a .com or .net domain will usually cost £30 or more).

It's important to buy your domain name from a reputable company, partly so that you can be sure you really have got the rights to it, and partly because if the company goes out of business it's just possible that you won't get a renewal reminder and your domain name could go back into the pool to be bought by someone else. Here are some well-established companies to consider:

- **NetNames** at
  http://www.netnames.co.uk

- **DomainsNet** at
  http://www.domainsnet.com (Fig 9.2)

- **UK Reg** at http://www.ukreg.com

Each of these sites gives plenty of straightforward information about the process and the services available. In a nutshell, you start by choosing a name (such as 'dodgygoods'), then pick one or more top-level domains (such as .com), and then check to see whether the chosen combination is available. (Don't include a 'www.' prefix: that's only used in the

+info

Top-level domain
A domain name comes in two parts:
the unique name ('dodgygoods') and a
suffix (.com, .net, .org, .co.uk, and so on).
This suffix is called the top-level domain
(TLD). The four I just mentioned are the
well-established TLDs for UK users, but
from June 2001 it should be possible to
register domains for seven more TLDs:
.aero, .biz, .coop, .info, .museum, .name and
.pro. The .eu TLD should also be available
soon. Bear in mind that some TLDs are
restricted to limited companies, govern-
ments, and so on.

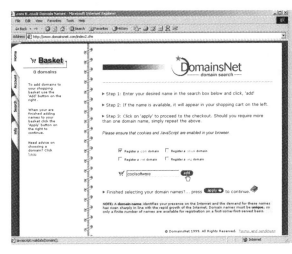

Figure 9.2
At DomainsNet, just type a name, pick a TLD, and click **Add** to add it to the shopping basket. If it's not available, a message will tell you.

address of your Web site, it's not a part of the domain name.) If your chosen combination hasn't been snapped up by someone else, you can slap your money on the table and register it.

Domain name transfer and forwarding

Once you've registered your domain name, you can do one of two things. One is to ask your ISP or hosting company to **transfer** the name to your Web space. You won't usually be able to do this if you're getting Web space for free, and some pay-for hosting companies will charge for the service. The other option is to use the registration company's **forwarding** service. Most registration companies offer this service, and few charge for it.

The way forwarding works is that after registering the name, you fill in a form that gives your current Web URL and your preferred email address. You tell everyone your snappy new URL (www. dodgygoods.com) and email address (me@dodgygoods.com), and the registration company's servers automatically forward visitors to your Web site and redirect email messages to the email address you gave.

The benefits of using Web forwarding services are twofold. First, it's quick and easy, and it saves you money if your host charges for domain transfers. Second, if you decide to switch to a different ISP or hosting company later on, you can simply visit the registration company's site and change the forwarding details.

Getting a free redirect URL

If you don't fancy spending money on a domain name, there's another option that works in a similar way to Web forwarding, but it's completely free. If you visit http://www.v3.com (Fig. 9.3), you can choose a URL along the lines of come.to/dodgygoods or surf.to/dodgygoods, and enter the real URL of your Web site. Give out the new, snappy URL to everyone you know, and visitors will automatically be redirected to your site.

Figure 9.3

Surf to V3 and choose a free short URL like surf.to/mysite.

Uploading your site

When you're ready to put your site on the Web, you'll use a system called **FTP** (File Transfer Protocol). FTP is one of the two major systems used to transfer files around the Internet, along with HTTP. The HTTP system is used for the Web, but it can only be used for *downloading* files (sending Web pages to your browser, for instance, which is why Web URLs begin with http://). FTP can be used to download files, but it can also *upload* them – send them to a remote server – which is what you need to do.

This is one of the few tricks your browser can't easily do, so you need to get your hands on an FTP program. Here are a few of the best:

- **FTP Explorer** from http://www.ftpx.com
- **CuteFTP** from http://www.cuteftp.com
- **WS_FTP Professional** from http://www.ipswitch.com

I'm going to assume you're using FTP Explorer, but most FTP programs look and work in much the same way. When you install FTP Explorer, it will offer to create a set of *Profiles* for you. These are links

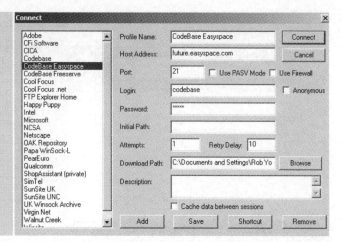

Figure 9.4

Creating a new profile for your Web space in FTP Explorer.

to FTP sites you can visit, a lot like browsers' Favorites and Bookmarks lists, so it's worth saying yes to this offer. You'll be prompted to enter your email address the first time you use the program, but you shouldn't need to change anything else.

Creating a profile

Your hosting company or ISP should have given you all the details you need to log into your Web space – a username, a password, and an FTP host address. The first job is to create a 'profile' for the site so that you can log in with a couple of clicks any time you want to make changes, so follow these steps:

1 Start FTP Explorer and, if you don't see the Connect dialog (shown in Fig. 9.4), choose **Connect** from the Tools menu. Click the **Add** button to create a new blank profile.

2 In the **Profile Name** box, type any name that you'll recognise as being your own site.

3 Type the FTP host address you were given into the **Host Address** box. If the address includes a path (forward slashes and directory names) only use the host name itself – the part before the first forward slash.

4 As this isn't a public FTP site that you log into anonymously, remove the checkmark from the **Anonymous** box then type your username and password in the **Login** and **Password** boxes.

5 If you had to leave out path details from the address in step 3, type that path into the **Initial Path** box, starting with the first forward slash. This is the directory that FTP Explorer should open when it connects to the host.

6 Click the **Save** button, and you'll see the new profile appear in the list to the left.

You're ready to upload!

With your FTP profile created (or the equivalent in your chosen FTP program), you're ready to publish your site to the Web. Select this profile in the Connect dialog's list and click the **Connect** button. In a few seconds you should be logged into your Web space and you'll see a two-pane view that will be familiar to Windows users: directories are shown in the left pane, with the contents of the current directory shown on the right. At the moment, of course, you won't see much there at all!

Find the 'Site' directory on your hard disk containing all the files belonging to your Web site and open it so that you can see the files and directories it contains. Select its entire contents and drag-and-drop them into FTP Explorer's window (Fig. 9.5). This is the simplest way to upload – it saves you having to remember which files you've uploaded and which you haven't. FTP Explorer will copy all the files to your Web space one by one, creating new directories as needed, and you can just sit back and watch. (Some FTP programs don't allow drag-and-drop, or won't let you drop directories, so you might have to click a button to create a directory with the same name as one in your 'Site' directory, and then upload the files it contains.)

If you need to create a new folder manually in FTP Explorer, just right-click on a blank area in the main window, choose **New** and **Folder**, and type a name. You can then just double-click this new folder to open it and start copying files into it.

Figure 9.5

Drop your site's files and directories into FTP Explorer, then make coffee while it all happens for you!

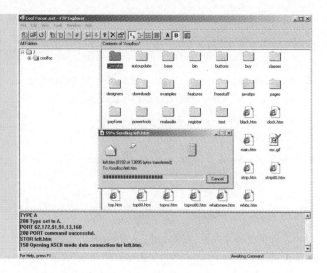

FTP transfer modes

*Most FTP programs give you a choice between two transfer modes, **ASCII** and **Binary** (FTP Explorer has buttons labelled A and B on its toolbar for this). ASCII mode can only be used to transfer plain text files, and will do so a tiny bit faster than Binary mode, which has to be used for any other type of file (zip files, images, programs, and so on). Since text files tend to be small anyway, the time saved by using ASCII mode is negligible, and you'd probably spend more time choosing and switching modes than you could ever save! It's simplest to stick with Binary mode for everything.*

Testing your site

This is the big one! Fire up your browser, type the URL of your Web site into its address bar and press **Enter**, and you should see its index page. If you don't, take a look at the troubleshooting tips below. If you do, congratulations!

Now you need to calm down, get a grip, and do a thorough test of every page, every link, and every item of content. It's not unusual to find that odd things have 'broken' in the transfer from hard disk to Web, and you may need to do some fixing. Along with testing all your internal links (and 'hidden' links such as external style sheets), remember to check links to other sites. At last you'll be able to judge the speed of your site too.

Testing a site is a vital step, not only when you first upload it, but whenever you add or alter pages – you can make a whole page of content disappear just by missing out a closing script, style or comment tag, forgetting a closing quote, or deleting a > symbol!

Troubleshooting

If everything goes right first time, your site will work just as well online as it worked on your hard disk. Just in case you hit a snag, though, here are a few troubleshooting tips to help you sort it out. If you need to make changes to a page, remember to change the copy on your hard disk. You can then upload that to the same online directory to replace the original version. Similarly, if you rename an online file using your FTP program, rename the copy on your hard disk too – keeping both copies of the site identical will help your future maintenance.

'I can't see my site!'
First, make sure you've typed your URL correctly and you really are online. Next, check that the HTML file that should form the front page of your site can be found – try including it in the URL like this: http://www.mysite.com/index.htm. If the page loads, that means that your Web server uses a different default filename, such as default.htm, which your hosting company can tell you. If so, rename the file on your hard disk and use your FTP program to rename the online copy.

'My links don't work!'
Make sure none of the files you're linking to has a space in its name. If you find a space, rename the local and online copies of the files to remove the space, and edit any pages linking to it. Next, check that you haven't used any upper-case letters in links that don't appear in the filenames (or vice versa). On the majority of Web servers, filenames are case-sensitive. Finally, of course, make sure you really have uploaded the files you're linking to, and that they're in the same relative location online as they are on your hard disk.

'Everything takes ages to download!'

That may be a problem of page-weight: using the hard-disk copy of your site, look at the size of the HTML file and any images, applets, scripts and other content that it links to, and add up the sizes. If the page loads a frameset, remember that it's actually loading two or more pages and all their content. Try experimenting with the images to see if you can reduce their size, or cut down the amount of content by splitting a large single page into two smaller linked pages. Of course, the problem may be that your host's server is slow (either temporarily or chronically), a common problem, especially with free hosting.

'Part of the page has disappeared!'

This usually has an easy answer: a closing tag has gone missing! Check the offending page for `<SCRIPT>`, `<STYLE>`, `<APPLET>` and other content-related tags and make sure that each has a matching closing tag (such as `</STYLE>`). If the pages uses tables, make sure you have a closing `</TABLE>` tag and that every `<TD>` and `<TR>` tag is closed before the next cell or row begins.

'The links open in a new window instead of a frame!'

This means that the `TARGET` attribute of the `<A>` tag is set to a frame name that doesn't exist. Compare the name in that attribute with the names in the `<FRAME>` tags of your frame-setting page: you've probably spelt the name wrongly in one or the other, or used an upper-case letter that should be lower-case.

Hitting the publicity trail

So you have a Web site, and it works. Now you want people to come and visit it, so you need to let them know it exists. One method is to contact the authors of sites covering similar subjects and ask if they'd like to exchange links – you add links to their sites in return for links to yours.

Another method is to use banner advertising. A handy free service called Banner Exchange operates in a similar way to the link exchange suggestion above: in return for displaying other members'

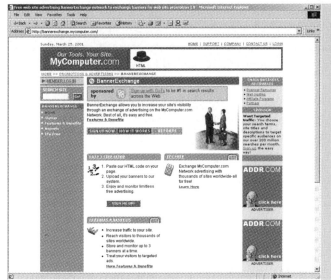

Figure 9.6

Visit Banner Exchange
to trade free
advertising space with
other members.

advertising banners on your own site, your ads will be displayed on theirs. The more pages you're willing to include a banner on, the more your own banners will be shown. If you want to use this method, visit one of the sites below, fill in the online forms, add the HTML code generated by the service to your pages, and then upload your own banners.

- **Banner Exchange** at http://bannerexchange.mycomputer.com (Fig. 9.6)

- **UK Banners** at http://www.ukbanners.com

- **Link Exchange** at http://store.bcentral.com/le/index.html

Another vital step in promoting a Web site is to try to get it listed with the major search engines. Because search engines work in different ways, this is a two-step process. Some search engines use a software 'robot' that scours the Web for new sites and indexes them by reading their pages, so the first step is to make some changes to your site to make it 'search engine-friendly'. Other engines only index a site when you ask to have it included, so the second step is to manually submit your site to as many search engines as you can.

For the first of those steps, begin by making a list of the important keywords and short phrases that describe your site – the words that you think people will type into a search engine when looking for a site like yours. Aim for between 10 and 20 keywords, putting the most important words first. Next, write a description of your site (using up to about 100 words), trying to include your most important keywords in the description. Finally, add the keywords and description to the head section of your site's index page using <META> tags like this:

```
<META NAME="keywords"CONTENT="keyword1,keyword2,
keyword3,keyword4">

<META NAME="description"CONTENT="A description of
my page, including a few keywords, that could be
shown in the search results.">
```

Make sure that the titles of your pages (between the <TITLE> and </TITLE> tags) are as meaningful as possible and try to include at least one of your keywords. It also helps if the first paragraph of text on your index page is reasonably descriptive and appetising.

After you've made your site more search engine-friendly and uploaded the edited pages to your site, it's time to embark on the second step – the manual submissions. As there are literally hundreds of search engines on the Web, this is a job that could take forever, but fortunately you don't need to visit every single one personally. The vast majority of search engine-introduced hits come from the five big players, Yahoo!, Google, Excite, AltaVista, and Lycos, and they give preference to sites that have been submitted manually, so visit those first and take your time filling in the details. At each site, look for a link marked **Submit URL**, **Add Your Site** or something similar (usually a small link at the foot of the page), and then follow the instructions.

When you've taken care of the major search engines, you may not have the time or patience to visit dozens of smaller engines, read their rules and fill in their forms. If not, there are services available that can do this for you. You just fill in a single form, then follow a step-by-step process to submit to several sites. Along the way you'll be prompted for any extra information needed by a particular site (such as picking a subject category) without repeatedly entering the same information. Here are three free services to start you off:

- **AddMe** at http://www.addme.com submits your site to 25 search engines

- **CNET Search.com** at http://www.search.com submits to up to 15 engines (Fig. 9.7)

- **Submit Express** at http://www.submitexpress.com will submit to 40 search sites

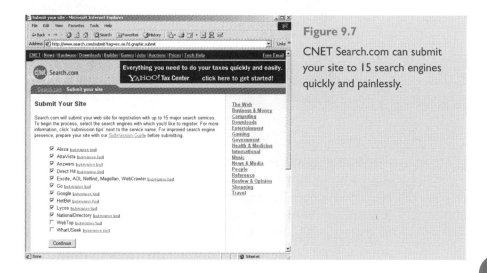

Figure 9.7

CNET Search.com can submit your site to 15 search engines quickly and painlessly.

So... has it worked?

With your promotion underway you obviously need some way of knowing how many people are actually visiting your site – at the very least you need a hit counter. But why settle for a simple tally of the number of visitors to a particular page when you can get a complete statistical analysis? As you've probably come to expect, this is something you can get for free.

Figure 9.8

WebSTAT.com can tell
you everything you
want to know about
who's visiting your site,
when, and how.

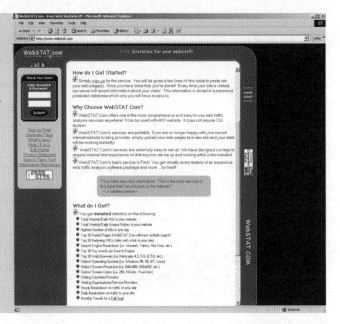

Two of the best site-stats services are at http://www.webstat.com
(Fig. 9.8) and http://www.thecounter.com. At either of these, sign up for
a free account, entering your site's URL and your email address, and
you'll receive a small chunk of HTML code in return. Place this code
at the bottom of your site's index page, and every visitor's details will
be logged by the service. At any time you can log in to your account
and check how many hits you're getting, where they're coming from,
which browsers they're using, and lots more. Even if it's not all actually *useful*, you'll find it fascinating.

What do *you* think?

As a Webmaster, your number one resource is your audience – if
they like what you've got, you're on to a winner; if they don't, you
lose. So an important part of running a Web site is to encourage visitors to give you feedback, and there are two good ways to do this.

The first is to make sure you've made email links easily accessible (see Chapter 3), either by placing them on every page or by adding a Contact Us link to your site's main navigation panel.

The second method is to add a guestbook to the site. Visitors can visit the guestbook page to read the comments left by others and add their own at the click of a link. As with so much in Web life, guestbooks are something you can find for free. Two services worth a look are Guestbook4free.com at http://www.guestbook4free.com (Fig. 9.9) and TheGuestbook at http://www.theguestbook.com, but a search for 'guestbook+free' at any search engine should turn up links to others.

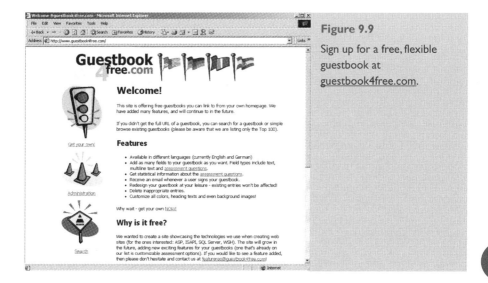

Figure 9.9

Sign up for a free, flexible guestbook at guestbook4free.com.

Appendix A
HTML colour names

AliceBlue
AntiqueWhite
Aqua
Aquamarine
Azure
Beige
Bisque
Black
BlanchedAlmond
Blue
BlueViolet
Brown
Burlywood
CadetBlue
Chartreuse
Chocolate
Coral
CornflowerBlue
Cornsilk
Crimson
Cyan
DarkBlue
DarkCyan
DarkGoldenrod
DarkGray
DarkGreen
DarkKhaki
DarkMagenta
DarkOliveGreen

DarkOrange
DarkOrchid
DarkRed
DarkSalmon
DarkSeaGreen
DarkSlateBlue
DarkSlateGray
DarkTurquoise
DarkViolet
DeepPink
DeepSkyBlue
DimGray
DodgerBlue
Firebrick
FloralWhite
ForestGreen
Fuchsia
Gainsboro
GhostWhite
Gold
Goldenrod
Gray
Green
GreenYellow
Honeydew
HotPink
IndianRed
Indigo
Ivory

Khaki
Lavender
LavenderBlush
LawnGreen
LemonChiffon
LightBlue
LightCoral
LightCyan
LightGoldenrodYellow
LightGreen
LightGray
LightPink
LightSalmon
LightSeaGreen
LightSkyBlue
LightSlateGray
LightSteelBlue
LightYellow
Lime
LimeGreen
Linen
Magenta
Maroon
MediumAquamarine
MediumBlue
MediumOrchid
MediumPurple
MediumSeaGreen
MediumSlateBlue
MediumSpringGreen
MediumTurquoise
MediumVioletRed
MidnightBlue
MintCream
MistyRose
Moccasin
NavajoWhite
Navy
OldLace
Olive
OliveDrab

Orange
OrangeRed
Orchid
PaleGoldenrod
PaleGreen
PaleTurquoise
PaleVioletRed
PapayaWhip
PeachPuff
Peru
Pink
Plum
PowderBlue
Purple
Red
RosyBrown
RoyalBlue
SaddleBrown
Salmon
SandyBrown
SeaGreen
Seashell
Sienna
Silver
SkyBlue
SlateBlue
SlateGray
Snow
SpringGreen
SteelBlue
Tan
Teal
Thistle
Tomato
Turquoise
Violet
Wheat
White
WhiteSmoke
Yellow
YellowGreen

Appendix B
Useful Web sites

HTML and general reference

Web site	URL
Bare Bones Guide to HTML	webach.com/barebones
BrowserWatch	browserwatch.internet.com
Cnet.com – Web Building	www.cnet.com/webbuilding
Facts & Stats	www.dotcom.com/facts /quickstats.html
Freesite UK	www.freesiteuk.com
HTML Code Help	www.netmechanic.com
HTML Goodies	www.htmlgoodies.com
The HTML Writers Guild	www.hwg.org
ISP Review	www.ispreview.co.uk
Searchterms.com – The Top 10	www.searchterms.com
SiteExperts.com	www.siteexperts.com
StatMarket	www.statmarket.com
W3C – World Wide Web Consortium	www.w3.org
WebDeveloper.com	www.webdeveloper.com
Web Developer's Virtual Library	www.wdvl.com
WebMonkey	hotwired.lycos.com/webmonkey
WebReference	www.webreference.com
webresource.net: HTML Center	www.webresource.net/html
WebSiteGoodies	www.websitegoodies.com
Web Site Garage	www.websitegarage.com
yesWebmaster.com	www.yeswebmaster.com

Graphics

Web site	URL
Absolutely Free Backgrounds	www.free-backgrounds.com
Abstract Dimensions PSP Filters	psptips.com/filters
Andrew's GraphXKingdom	www.graphxkingdom.com
ArtToday.com	www.arttoday.com
bannerblast.com	www.bannerblast.com
Clipart.com	www.clipart.com
ClipArtConnection.com	www.clipartconnection.com
CoolText.com	www.cooltext.com
Corbis	www.corbis.com
Filter Factory Plug-ins	showcase.netins.net/web/ wolf359/plugins.htm
Free Graphics	www.freegraphics.com
Free Images	www.freeimages.co.uk
HitBox Image Search	hitbox.gograph.com
IconBazaar	www.iconbazaar.com
Jeffrey Zeldman Presents	www.zeldman.com
MediaBuilder	www.mediabuilder.com
PhotoDisc	www.photodisc.com
ScreamDesign	www.screamdesign.com
Textureland	www.textureland.com
webresource.net: Graphics Center	www.webresource.net/ graphics
yesWebMaster.com Graphics	www.yeswebmaster. com/graphics

Flash

Web site	URL
ExtremeFlash	www.extremeflash.com
Flahoo	www.flahoo.com
Flash Kit	www.flashkit.com
Flash Planet	www.flashplanet.com

Macromedia	www.macromedia.com
ShockFusion	www.shockfusion.com
shockwave.com	www.shockwave.com

JavaScript

Web site	URL
Cut-N-Paste JavaScript	www.infohiway.com/ javascript/indexf.htm
Dynamic Drive	www.dynamicdrive.com
JavaScript.com	www.javascript.com
JavaScript City	www.javascriptcity.com
JavaScript Search	www.javascriptsearch.com
JavaScript Source	javascript.internet.com
JavaScript Tip of the Week	www.webreference. com/javascript
JavaScript World	www.jsworld.com
WebCoder.com	www.webcoder.com
webresource.net: JavaScript Center	www.webresource. net/javascript

Dynamic HTML

Web site	URL
Comet Cursor	www.cometcursors.com
DHTML Lab	www.webreference.com/dhtml
Dynamic HTML Developer Zone	www.projectcool.com/devel oper/dynamic
Dynamic Drive	www.dynamicdrive.com
Dynamic HTML Resource	www.htmlguru.com
Dynamic HTML Zone	www.dhtmlzone.com
Experience DHTML!	www.bratta.com/dhtml
MSDN Online Voices	msdn.microsoft.com/ voices/dude.asp
WebCoder.com	www.webcoder.com

Java

Web site	URL
Cool Focus	www.coolfocus.com
Gamelan	softwaredev.earthweb.com/java
JARS	www.jars.com
JavaSoft (Sun)	www.javasoft.com
The Java Boutique	javaboutique.internet.com
webresource.net: Java Center	www.webresource.net/java

Guestbooks, counters and statistics

Web site	URL
1-2-3 WebTools	www.freeguestbooks.com
Beseen Free Web Tools	www.beseen.com
Guestbook4free.com	www.guestbook4free.com
GuestBooks.net	www.glacierweb.com/home
HitBox.com	www.hitbox.com
I-Count	www.icount.com
MyComputer.com	guestbook.mycomputer.com
RealTracker Free	www.showstat.com
theCounter.com	www.thecounter.com
theGuestBook.com	www.theguestbook.com
WebTracker	www.fxweb.holowww. com/tracker
XOOMCounter	www2.pagecount.com
ZapZone	www.zzn.com

Forums, chat and other content

Web site	URL
Ballot-Box.net	www.ballot-box.net
BeSeen Bulletin Board	www.beseen.com/board
BeSeen Enhance: Quizlet	www.beseen.com/quiz

BeSeen Chat	www.beseen.com/chat
BoardHost	www.boardhost.com
EZBoard	www.ezboard.com
EZPolls	ezpolls.mycomputer.com
Free Forums	www.freeforums.com
Free Site Search Engine	www.freefind.com
Free Tools	www.freetools.com
liveuniverse.com	liveuniverse.com
Mister Poll	www.misterpoll.com
Multicity.com	www.multicity.com
NetVotes	www.netvotes.com
ParaChat	www.parachat.com
PollIt	www.pollit.com
QuickChat	www.quickchat.org
Web BBS	awsd.com/scripts/webbbs
ZapZone	www.zzn.com

Domain name registration

Web site	URL
DomainBook.com	www.domainbook.com
Domains365	www.domains365.co.uk
DomainsNet	www.domainsnet.co.uk
interNIC	www.internic.net
NetNames	www.netnames.co.uk
Simply Names	www.simplynames.co.uk
UK Reg	www.ukreg.com

Web site promotion, marketing and advertising

Web site	URL
AddMe	www.addme.com
AdValue	www.advalue.co.uk

BannerExchange	bannerexchange. mycomputer.com
Bpath	www.bpath.com
DoubleClick	www.doubleclick.com
GoTo Search Suggestions	inventory.goto.com/inventory/ Search_Suggestion.jhtml
EReleases	www.ereleases.com
Internet Advertising Bureau	www.iab.net
Internet PR Guide	www.internetprguide.com
JimTools	www.jimtools.com
Microsoft bCentral	www.bcentral.com
Refer-It.com	www.refer-it.com
SearchAbility	www.searchability.com
Search Engine Watch	www.searchenginewatch.com
Submit Corner	www.submitcorner.com
Submit Express	www.submitexpress.com
Submit It!	www.submit-it.com
SubmitWizard	submitwizard.mycomputer.com
TopWeb site	www.topweb site.co.uk
ukaffiliates.com	www.ukaffiliates.com
UK Banners	www.ukbanners.com
ValueClick	www.valueclick.com/uk
WebPromote	www.webpromote.com
WEBpromotion.co.uk	www.webpromotion.co.uk
Web Site Garage	register-it.netscape.com

Cool site collections and awards

Web site	URL
Cool Central	www.coolcentral.com
Cybersmith's Hot Site of the Day	www.cybersmith.com/hotsites
Dr Webster's Site of the Day	www.drwebster.com
Family Site of the Day	www.worldvillage.com/ famsite.htm
Hot 100 Web sites	www.web21.com

Too Cool!	www.toocool.com
Webby Awards	www.webbyawards.com
Web Pages That Suck	www.webpagesthatsuck.com
World Best Web sites	www.worldbestweb sites.com
Xplore's Site of the Day	www.xplore.com

Shareware directories

Web site	URL
32bit.com	www.32bit.com/software
DaveCentral	www.davecentral.com
Jumbo	www.jumbo.com
KeyScreen	www.keyscreen.com
MacShare.com	www.macshare.com
NoNags	www.nonags.com
Shareware.com	www.shareware.com
Thingamabobs	www.thingamabobs.com
Tucows	tucows.mirror.ac.uk
WinSite	www.winsite.com
ZDNet Downloads	www.zdnet.com/downloads

Search engines

Web site	URL
All The Web	www.alltheweb.com
AltaVista	www.altavista.com
AOL Search	search.aol.com
Ask Jeeves	www.ask.com
Canada.com	www.canada.com
CNET Search.com	www.search.com
Direct Hit	www.directhit.com
Dogpile	www.dogpile.com
Excite	www.excite.com
Galaxy	www.galaxy.com

GO.com	www.go.com
Go2Net	www.gotonet.com
Google	www.google.com
GoTo.com	www.goto.com
HotBot	www.hotbot.com
ICQ Search	www.icqit.com
InfoSpace	www.infospace.com
LookSmart	www.looksmart.com
Lycos	www.lycos.com
Mamma.com	www.mamma.com
MetaCrawler	www.metacrawler.com
Mirago	www.mirago.co.uk
MSN	search.msn.com
NationalDirectory	www.nationaldirectory.com
NBCi	www.nbci.com
Netscape Search	search.netscape.com
Northern Light	www.northernlight.com
OneSeek	www.oneseek.com
Open Directory Project	www.dmoz.org
ProFusion	www.profusion.com
Scrub The Web	www.scrubtheweb.com
Search Engine Colossus	www.searchenginecolossus.com
Search UK	uk.searchengine.com
Starting Point	www.stpt.com
UK Plus	www.ukplus.co.uk
WebCrawler	www.webcrawler.com
WebTop.com	www.webtop.com
WebZone	www.infohiway.com
whatUseek	www.whatuseek.com
Yahoo!	www.yahoo.com

index